Social
Psychology

A BRIEF INTRODUCTION

Social Psychology

A BRIEF INTRODUCTION

JOSEPH E. McGRATH
University of Illinois

Holt, Rinehart and Winston
NEW YORK / CHICAGO / SAN FRANCISCO
TORONTO / LONDON

4 5 6 7 8 9

Preface

This book is intended to give a brief but structured over-view of the field of social psychology. It is not comprehensive, as it would have to be many times as large to give even a bare-bones presentation of all research and theory in social psychology. The purpose is, rather, to present the major concepts of the field and relate them to one another in a meaningful pattern.

The book is eclectic in that it draws concepts and hypotheses from various theoretical schools rather than presenting all material from a single theoretical position. At the same time it is built around a general frame of reference which is designed to help the student see how concepts drawn from diverse sources are related to one another.

Though brief, this presentation is not in any sense an attempt to pop-ularize social-psychological knowledge. It does not seek to show how social-psychological findings can be applied to the solution of social prob-lems or to the enhancement of personal adjustment. It deals with social psychology as a basic science and attempts to present the current state of development of social psychology as a science as accurately as possible. It does not contain a pat statement of "the laws of social behavior," be-cause no such laws have, as yet, been firmly established and verified. Many more questions are posed than resolved, in accordance with the current status of the field. The aim is, above all, to give the student a perspective about the application of scientific method (that is, systematic inquiry) to the study of human social behavior—to show how scientific in-quiry proceeds, what it has accomplished to date, and what its limitations as well as its possibilities are for the future.

The book is designed to serve in any of three capacities: (1) as a core textbook for an introductory course in social psychology, to be supplemented by additional readings; (2) as one of a series of brief textbooks for various interdisciplinary courses in the behavioral sciences which include but are not limited to the field of social psychology; (3) as a general overview and introduction to the literature of the field for graduate and advanced undergraduate students in other fields who wish to develop a working knowledge of social psychology. For any of these uses, the lists of supplementary readings given at the end of each part of the book should be helpful guides.

Many people contribute to the development of a book, and this one is no exception. There is not enough space to cite all by name, but at least three sets of people deserve special acknowledgment and an expression of my gratitude. First, I want to thank the students of my Psychology 101 classes at the University of Illinois, who have "pretested" various preliminary versions of the textbook and whose feedback has made it possible to expand, clarify, and otherwise improve the book. Secondly, I am grateful for the help of several teaching assistants, whose constructive criticism has greatly improved both the quality of the course and of this manuscript: Lynn Anderson, Doyle Bishop, Lester Cooper, B. B. McCaa, William McDonald, William Meuwese, Josephine Naidoo, and Larry VanEgeren. The third group, whose contributions I especially wish to acknowledge, are my professional colleagues, past and present. While many have contributed to this effort, directly and indirectly, special thanks go to two whose contributions literally made it possible to complete this book. The first is Prof. T. M. Newcomb. As my mentor of many years, he has greatly influenced my knowledge and interpretation of the field of social psychology; as editor of this book, he has improved the manuscript immensely. The second is Prof. P. J. Runkle. As my friend and colleague for many years, his frank and incisive criticism, as well as his encouragement, have contributed much both to my general education and to the quality of this work. While the errors and inadequacies are my own responsibility, I must share credit for its positive merits with these and many others who have helped me plan and write this book.

Joseph E. McGrath

Urbana, Illinois
May 1964

Contents

PART ONE /

The Science of

Social Psychology

Social psychology is the study of how human behavior is influenced by the presence, behavior, and products of other human beings, individually and collectively, past, present, and future. We are all social psychologists in a sense, since everyone is aware that people influence one another; we all take part in such influence processes, and most of us have some "theories" about how interpersonal influence operates. In the same sense, we are all meteorologists when we notice that storm clouds are approaching and that barometric pressure is falling and predict rain. We are all physicists when we recognize that gravity, friction, and momentum influence the behavior of our car when we turn it at high speed. And we are all political scientists when we read about, discuss, and participate in the political process. However, no one would claim to be an expert in the science of meteorology or the science of physics on the basis of such meager knowledge of the concepts and principles of those fields and without formal education in those disciplines. Similarly, while we are all involved in the *phenomena* of social psychology and often need information about those phenomena (e.g., we would often find it useful to understand and predict the behavior of others), we are not thereby fully qualified experts in the science of social psychology.

Furthermore, as you have probably noticed, people frequently disagree about the "hows" and "whys" of human behavior. Even when people agree about human behavior, they may be collectively wrong in what they believe. The science of social psychology attempts to provide criteria for judging the correctness of statements about the social behavior of human beings and to expose ideas about human social behavior to the test of those criteria. This book is about social psychology as a science, that is, as the *systematic* study of social factors which affect human behavior.

The main concepts of the field of social psychology are dealt with in Parts Two, Three, and Four. Part One is concerned with some preliminary matters. Chapter 1 is a brief discussion of the nature of science and the place of social psychology in the family of sciences. Then, since any discipline is greatly affected by features of its own historical development, Chapter 2 reviews some major features in the history of social psychology which affect the current status of that field. The backbone of any science is its methodology. Hence, Chapter 3 presents a brief description of the methods by which social psychologists attempt to gain knowledge about their field of study.

Social psychology is a fairly new field of study and one that draws upon background concepts of several other fields—most notably, the fields of psychology, sociology, and anthropology. Because of its interdisciplinary nature and its recent and rapid development, the content of social psychology is quite heterogeneous and does not fall very neatly into subareas. To present a brief but systematic treatment of social psychology—which is the aim of this book—requires that we impose some organizing framework on the content of the field. The framework used here is implicit in the organization of Parts Two, Three, and Four. Its major features are outlined in the following paragraphs so as to provide a general frame of reference for approaching each part of the book and relating the parts to one another, even though some of the concepts mentioned here will not be fully clarified until later.

Social psychology deals with phenomena at each of three levels of analysis: the individual, the small groups of which he is a part, and the total society and culture within which he is embedded. These three levels are dealt with as separate but related foci in Parts Two, Three, and Four, which comprise the main substance of the book.

In Part Two we will consider how the development of the *individual* human being is affected by features of his social environment—other people with whom he is engaged in real and symbolic interaction. In Part Three we will shift our focus of concern to those relatively small, face-to-face *groups* that provide the main context for human interaction, and consider how such groups operate and how they influence the individuals who take part in them. Part Four shifts focus again, to a discussion of properties of the over-all social environment—the *total society* and *culture* within which the individual and his groups are embedded—as these shape the pattern of the individual's life and actions.

While these three levels can be clearly distinguished for analytic purposes, they are by no means unrelated. Groups are, after all, composed of individuals, and human interaction in groups is the interplay of behaviors of the set of individuals involved. Furthermore, the properties of the society and culture that influence the individual, which we will consider in Part Four, are the same social factors considered in Part Two as "translated" by the particular individuals and groups who take part in the process of development of any particular human being. Thus, from Part Two through Part Four we will come full circle, from a concern with the development of the individual as such, back to an analysis of the social factors which influence that development.

While concepts at the three levels are not entirely parallel, our treatment will be organized around certain formal similarities among the levels. At each level, there is a "unity," which is the focus of study: the individual; the group; and the culture and total society. We will be concerned with the *structure* of that unity at each level, that is, with the differentiation of its parts and the pattern of integration by which the parts form a whole. We will also be concerned with *processes*—differentiation, integration, disorganization, and others—by which the unity and its parts develop and change through time. Finally, we will be concerned with certain *substantively different* kinds of parts at each level; for example, with motives and attitudes at the individual level, with group goals and group norms at the group level. There are some parallels between the substantive distinctions at each level. In fact, the ancient Platonic triad of knowing (cognition), feeling (affection), and striving (conation) still comes quite close to identifying the main substantive classes of social psychological concepts at each level. At the individual level, for example, we will deal with perceptions and belief systems (cognition), with attitudes (affection), and with motivation (conation).

The reader must be warned, however, that this schema fits the material very roughly in many places. Cognitive, affective, and conative concepts are not given equal emphasis at each level; nor are these three facets of human behavior clearly distinguished in all social psychological concepts. For these reasons, we do not try to hold closely to our analytic distinctions (structure; process; and cognitive, affective, and conative concepts) in the chapter and section headings within each part of the book. To do so would require too much bending of the material to fit our oversimplified framework. Rather, these concepts are presented here—and used as an implicit structuring of subsequent materials—to give the reader a very general orientation as to how the book is organized and why.

CHAPTER 1

Social psychology as
an area of study

The scientific study of human behavior

As we observe other people in our daily lives, we are often struck by the variety and complexity of human behavior. Each person we know is somehow different from every other person we have ever met. No two people seem to have just the same talents, attitudes, or ways of behaving. Each person is unique.

Yet at the same time we often notice striking similarities among certain people. We may notice, for example, that there are certain similarities in the behavior of people who live in cities as compared with those who live in rural areas; or among people from a certain region of the country; or people in certain occupations—bankers or barbers or physicians; or people of a given ethnic, religious, or racial background. While almost everyone would agree that such uniformities exist, it is likely that there would be much disagreement as to what the uniformities are and what factors (i.e., race, region, occupation, or others) give rise to them.

The basic aim of the social sciences is to identify such underlying regularities in human behavior—both similarities and differences—and to determine what antecedent conditions give rise to them and what consequences follow from them. The differences between deliberate research activities of the social scientist and casual observations and conclusions of the sophisticated layman are mainly matters of *procedure* or *method*. They have to do with how clearly and precisely a person formulates his concepts, how carefully and systematically he makes and records observations, and how rigorous is the logic by which he reasons from data to conclusions. The differences are really differences in degree, but it is precisely these that separate science from folklore in physics, astronomy, and biology, as well as in social psychology and other social sciences.

Many of the basic questions of the social sciences are nearly as ancient as man himself: What is basic to human nature—what is man *really* like? Are all men basically alike and only superficially different, or are differences among them basic? How does man become the way he is? Is his basic nature "built in," or does he change through experience? If the latter, what kind of experiences make what kind of men?

What differences are there between men and women, between races, between ethnic groups? Are such differences inherent, or are they the results of experience? Are all the people of one group (say, all men or all women) alike, while that group differs from another, or is there variation within each group as well as between groups?

Answers to these basic questions—though not necessarily correct answers—are also as old as man himself, because these are compelling questions. The business of living requires that we *assume* some set of answers to these questions in order to be able to interact effectively with the people around us. In fact, every individual operates all the time on the basis of some set of assumptions about man and his nature, although many may never make such a philosophy of life explicit. Thus, the basic impetus for social science, from ancient times, has been man's need to understand his own behavior and the behavior of others.

Early answers to questions about man and his nature were speculative rather than scientific. Early social philosophers were handicapped by two conditions. First, each individual "theorist" was largely dependent on his own observations and reasoning, as there did not exist much of a body of recorded information or ideas for him to draw on. Secondly, his own observations were likely to be very limited—in time, space, and quantity. Thus, early thinkers were not in a position to separate the general properties that apply to all humans, or broad categories of them, from particular properties of the men and situations which they encountered more or less accidentally in their daily lives. These two limitations existed for early philosophers, who dealt with the nature of the physical world, as well as for social philosophers. Many centuries later man's efforts to understand human nature shifted from the early forms of speculation to a systematic empirical approach modeled largely after the approach that had already proved very successful in the study of physical phenomena. The course of these developments will be discussed in Chapter 2. We will turn now to the question of the nature of science and how various sciences relate to one another.

The social sciences as sciences

Science is the systematic attempt to describe, interrelate, explain, and hence predict some set of phenomena. The phenomena must have some empirical referent; that is, they must be observable or lead to observable effects. Within that limit, what is science and what is not depends not on the content of the phenomena but on the methods by which the phenomena are studied.

An area of study can be more or less scientific to the extent that it meets four general criteria:

1. OBJECTIVITY OF VIEWPOINT: The scientist must be unbiased regarding the outcome of his study. He must not have a vested interest in proving any particular answer to the question he poses, only a vested interest in identifying or approaching the "true" answer.
2. EXPLICIT PROCEDURES THAT CAN BE REPLICATED: He must state in explicit terms just what he did to obtain his data, just what logical and arithmetic operations he performed on these data to reach the results he reports, and by what steps of reasoning he got from his raw results to his interpretation of them.
3. RELIABLE MEASUREMENT: He must utilize some means for discerning the presence or absence of the phenomena he is studying and for measuring the intensity or magnitude of those phenomena under controlled and/or known conditions.
4. SOUND LOGIC: He must use a sound and explicit logic in planning and conducting his study, and in the way he reasons from results to conclusions.

Are the social sciences really sciences? Or are they academic disciplines more like the arts or the humanities, but trying to pass themselves off as sciences to take advantage of the current popularity and status accorded to scientific pursuits? The answer to this question, of course, depends on what is meant by the term "science." If you define science in terms of certain content areas, for example, the physical sciences, then of course nothing else fits the definition. However, if you define science in terms of method, as it is defined here, then it is legitimate to ask and try to answer the question: Are the social sciences scientific?

The most honest answer to this question seems to be that some areas are; some are not. To phrase it in another way, the different disciplines that are usually classified as social sciences vary in the degree to which they deal with a body of knowledge obtained through objective, replicable, and reliable measurement and sound logic of inference; hence, they vary in the degree to which we can consider them scientific.

The differences are not between disciplines, but rather among different parts of the same scientific field. Some parts of psychology, sociology, and economics are as scientific, by the above definition, as any of the physical sciences. Other parts of all three of these fields—while no less interesting and perhaps more useful in some respects—are still very inadequate as scientific endeavors because they are largely speculative and nonobjective, and involve nonreplicable, "intuitive" procedures rather than explicit and concrete ones.

It is sometimes argued that the hallmark of science is precision of quantitative measurement and the use of mathematical formulations. From this point of view, one might conclude that very little, if any, of so-called social science (and for that matter, only a portion of physical and biological science) is really scientific. There is some truth in this point of view; and the need for reliable observation (measurement) is one of the crucial criteria of scientific activity. However, one should not confuse the *form* in which data are recorded (for example, in numbers versus words) with their reliability (that is, how closely two observations of the same phenomena agree). All observations or measurements in all scientific fields have less than perfect reliability, regardless of whether they are recorded in numbers, words, or other symbols. However, the degree of precision and reliability of measurement varies greatly among the different areas of scientific inquiry. Hence, the areas in which measurement is more precise and reliable can reasonably be considered to be more scientific, in a relative sense, assuming that the other criteria of "scientificness" are adequately met.

Thus, the "scientificness" of any activity inheres in the methods of inquiry it uses. A general overview of methods used in social psychology is presented in Chapter 3. For a more complete discussion of social science research methods, see Festinger and Katz, 1953; or Selltiz et al., 1962, which are listed in the Supplementary Reading at the end of Part One.

Social psychology's place among the sciences

As implied in our definition of science, there are or can be sciences of many content areas. In classifying sciences it is useful to consider three main bodies of scientific endeavor:

1. PHYSICAL SCIENCES: Those that study the nonanimate substances and forces of the universe(s), for example, physics, chemistry, geology.
2. BIOLOGICAL SCIENCES: Those that study the animate forms in nature, plants, and animals, for example, botany, zoology, physiology.
3. SOCIAL SCIENCES: Those that study man as he relates to his fellow man, for example, sociology, economics, political science, anthropology.

In the physical sciences, man is the investigator and also one of the classes of objects which are subject to the forces and relationships under study, but not a specially important class of object in that respect. In the biological sciences, man is both investigator and one of the myriad species that are the objects of his study, and a rather important one. In the social sciences, man is both investigator and focus of study.

Philosophy, including logic and mathematics, is strictly speaking, not a science at all, but a metascience—a discipline underlying all the sciences. Mathematics is traditionally classed with the physical sciences, however, while different aspects of philosophy are variously classified.

Psychology is also a hybrid in this schema. It is partly a biological and partly a social science. We are concerned here with the social science aspect of psychology and to some extent with other social sciences as they shed light on our topic. Psychology deals with the behavior of human beings in relation to their environments. Social psychology is that part of psychology which is concerned with human behavior in relation to the social parts of the environment; that is, *social psychology deals with human behavior as it is influenced by the presence, beliefs, actions, and symbols of other men.*

Social psychology can also be considered as a special field within the science of sociology. General sociology deals with the forms and processes of collective behavior—behavior of men in the aggregate. Social psychology deals with the *articulation* between the individual, as an actor and as a target of effects, and larger social entities as they affect and are affected by individuals.

Thus, social psychology can be viewed either as a subfield within psychology or sociology, or as a linking or interdisciplinary field of study analogous to the field of biophysics. While it lies between psychology and sociology in the over-all pattern of sciences, it has historical roots in several other disciplines in addition to these fields.

CHAPTER 2

/ *Historical background of social psychology*

Every discipline is affected by its own past history. Many of the customs and emphases of current social psychology can be traced to the past, and even some of our current concepts are altered forms of ideas from much earlier times. In this chapter we will review briefly some of the major historical roots of social psychology, and examine some of the ways in which the field has changed in concepts and methodology.

Major historical roots

Certain aspects of modern social psychology can be traced back to at least five important predecessors. The history of social psychology as an area of formal inquiry probably began with the social philosophers of ancient Greece: Plato (427–347 B.C.), Aristotle (384–322 B.C.), the hedonists, and others. The field was further influenced many centuries later by philosophers of the British associationist school, such as Locke (1632–1704), Berkeley (1685–1753), Hume (1711–1776), Bentham (1748–1832), and James Mill (1773–1836). Basically, the social philosophers defined the key problems of the field: the nature of man, the nature of society, and the relation between the individual and society. They also provided various answers to these questions based on personal observation and speculation. These answers were usually single-factor theories that tried to explain the nature of man on the basis of one organizing concept (such as the "pleasure principle"). The social philosophers also tended to slip over the line between questions of "what is," the proper domain of science, and questions of "what ought to be," which are moral but not scientific questions. Nevertheless, the early social philosophers influenced the field greatly by the questions, observations, and conclusions they presented.

Another set of scholars who influenced social psychology were the early sociological theorists such as Comte (1798–1857), Le Bon (1841–1931), Durkheim (1858–1917), Simmel (1858–1918), Weber (1864–1920), G. H. Mead (1863–1931), and Cooley (1864–1929). Their major contributions were to insist on the reality of social phenomena and to point out the importance of collectivities in shaping the individual. Their work was important also in developing social psychology from a speculative social philosophy to an empirically oriented social science.

The field of medicine is another forerunner of modern social psychology, especially of the early forms of what would currently be called abnormal or clinical psychology. Early studies by Charcot (1825–1893) and Freud (1856–1939) of hypnosis and related phenomena led to the development of Freud's theories of how man's behavior is affected by irrational, unconscious forces within himself. Much of current social psychology deals with such irrational and unconscious forces in man, and places much emphasis on Freud's general concepts of personality, or modifications of them.

Cultural anthropology, too, had a major impact on social psychology. The early work of Boas (1858–1942) and later work by Margaret Mead (1901–   ), Ruth Benedict (1887–1948), and many others documented the wide diversity of types of social arrangements and the concomitant diversity of "human nature." Thus, they forced recognition that many features of human behavior thought to be biologically determined are neither universal nor innate.

Finally, the tremendous influence of experimental psychology on social psychology should be noted. The early experimental work of Wundt (1832–1920), Münsterberg (1863–1916), and many others showed the feasibility of using the classical laboratory experiment of the physical sciences as a method for the study of human behavior. Later, the behavioristic approach of Watson (1878–1958) and others placed emphasis on the use of objective measures of behavior. These two influences spread from experimental psychology to social psychology, and the experimental method of the physical sciences, with its accompanying control and precision of measurement, became the idealized method for social psychological research.

Changes in the bases of social-psychological work

Much has changed in the nature of social psychology since the early formulations of basic questions by the social philosophers. Many of the changes represent shifts in the basic philosophy of the field. These shifts in underlying philosophy transformed social psychology from a speculative to a scientific field and shaped the present nature of that field in many ways.

BASIS OF KNOWLEDGE

One crucial change from early times has been the assumption about how man gains knowledge. The social philosophers worked on the premise that man's "intuition," based on rational thought, provided a sound basis for "knowing." With the work of Comte, Watson, and others, there came a radical shift to what we would now call "raw empiricism." This view took the position that there can be no knowledge except that derived directly from sensory experience. In more recent times, social psychology has returned to a middle ground on this question, partly because of its own findings regarding man's sensory and perceptual behavior. Modern social psychologists generally view direct observation and experiment, on the one hand, and reasoning, on the other, as complementary procedures, both of which are needed for the accumulation of knowledge.

FORMS OF DATA

The early social philosophers based their conclusions on relatively limited observation plus rational thought. Later the main basis for gathering psychological data came to be systematic introspection: attempts by highly trained individuals to describe their own subjective experiences. When the Watson-inspired shift to behaviorism became dominant, such use of subjective data was rejected as outside the bounds of legitimate methodology, and emphasis was placed on systematic observation and measurement (preferably by an instrument) under highly controlled conditions. Currently, social psychologists make use of both objective (that is, observational) and subjective (that is, self-report) forms of data, as we shall see in Chapter 3.

COMPLEXITY OF FORMULATION

A shift has occurred in the kind of theoretical formulations used. Early workers usually formulated single-factor theories. Reaction against this oversimplification led to many-factor theories, which often were little more than catalogues of habits or sentiments or motives. Current theories, in reaction against both of these trends, usually present complex formulations based on multiple but highly interrelated variables. More and more, too, current theories of social psychology are utilizing the tools of mathematics to provide a rigorous language for the expression of theoretical concepts and their relationships.

SCIENTIFIC LAWS

A change has taken place in the kinds of "laws" or "principles" social scientists attempt to generate. The original emphasis was on formulation of totally general, usually simple, timeless laws, in the tradition of the physical sciences. As one-factor theories proved inadequate for explaining the variability and complexity of human behavior, emphasis shifted from the development of completely general laws to study of the individual case (person, group, culture). This latter emphasis is called the ideographic approach. It, too, proved unfeasible as a basis for a general science; following the ideographic position rigorously would yield as many distinct "psychologies" as there are individuals. But the ideographic approach established the importance of individual differences. Current social psychology tends to be nomothetic, that is, to seek general laws or relationships. But current social psychological relationships take into account the fact of individual differences and incorporate such differences and their causes as an integral part of theory.

PURPOSE OF SOCIAL SCIENCE

The underlying purpose of social psychology has shifted. The early philosophers tended to present moralistic (normative) views, views about "what ought to be" rather than "what is." As social psychology attempted to become a truly scientific field under the impetus of the ideas of Comte, Watson, F. Allport, Triplett, and others, it shifted to entirely descriptive, nonvaluative forms of concepts. In very recent times there has been some tendency toward a balancing of normative and descriptive approaches. This takes the form of applying the findings of social science for social action purposes. The relation between basic and applied emphases in social science is a fairly complex value question, and the issue is by no means resolved in current social psychology.

SPECIALIZATION

Specialization within the social sciences has increased tremendously, as it has in most other fields. In early times social philosophy represented an all-encompassing field of study, which subsumed all the present social sciences. As time advanced and knowledge grew, various fields came to be differentiated as separate disciplines requiring specialized training. Now we have not only psychology, sociology, political science, and many other separate fields within the social sciences but also a high degree of specialization within each of these fields. In psychology, for example, the physiological psychologist, the clinical psychologist, and the social psychologist have specialized educational programs and work on quite separate research activities. The high degree of fragmentation has led many to propose measures for broadening the educational experiences of the overspecialized scientist, to urge the development of interdisciplinary tools and concepts, and to propose that research be organized around particular problem areas rather than in terms of formal academic disciplines.

Some crucial controversies in the field

A number of theoretical issues have played a part in shaping current social psychology. Often reaction against an early, extreme position has led to an equally extreme counterposition. In such cases current theoretical positions usually represent an attempted synthesis of the extreme views. Three such controversies, or dilemmas, have had much historical significance in the field.

HEREDITY VERSUS ENVIRONMENT

Much of early social philosophy was based on the assumption that most human behavior is based on inherent hereditary factors and that regularities in human behavior are universal among mankind. The findings of cultural anthropology forced a recognition that there are vast differences in human behavior from one cultural setting to another. Hence, emphasis shifted from the position that man's behavior is to be understood in terms of universal hereditary principles to the position that much of man's behavior is learned and that what he learns depends on his environmental and cultural setting. Currently, most social psychologists resolve this issue by assuming that both heredity and environment are important causal bases for human behavior. The organism's biological endowment sets limits on the potential of that organism, while his interaction with his social environment provides the context for realization of that potential. Thus, effects of the social environment *interact* with hereditary factors in the development of the organism. Both heredity and environment shape man's behavior.

MAN AS RATIONAL VERSUS IRRATIONAL

The early social philosophers tended to assume that man's behavior is entirely or at least mainly rational. This view holds that man is fully aware of all the forces which affect his behavior, that he does what he does on the basis of deliberate choices, that he is reasonably intelligent and educable, and that he acts in a rational way which makes sense to others as well as to himself. Under the impetus of Freud's observations and theory, a contrary view of man came to be dominant in parts of psychology. This view holds that man's behavior is largely or wholly the result of blind instincts, drives, and emotions, of which he is usually not aware. What appears to be rational, cooperative, intelligent behavior is accounted for by the notion that man (unconsciously) tends to disguise his real motivations, clothing what would be socially unacceptable urges in the form of socially acceptable actions. Man's behavior is really "rational" in this view, too, in the sense of following a systematic and predictable pattern. But the basis of this rationality is blind, unconscious forces, rather than conscious, intelligent choices. Current social psychology has been much influenced by the Freudian view of behavior, especially in areas related to personality development. At the same time certain portions of the field (for example, much attitude and opinion measurement) still focus on the study of man's rational, conscious choice behavior.

INDIVIDUAL VERSUS SOCIETY

Social psychology has historical roots in both psychology and sociology, and in its early days the difference in orientation of these two fields led to a major cleavage in views within the field of social psychology. Psychologically oriented social psychologists, such as Floyd Allport, took the position that societies are derivatives of individuals and that social phenomena are to be accounted for on the basis of summations of properties of their constituent parts. Sometimes proponents of this view also argued for an extreme form of "reductionism," postulating that individual behavior must ultimately be explained in physiological terms. Sociologically oriented social psychologists, on the other hand, tended to take an emergent or holistic view rather than a reductionistic position. Many considered societies as the fundamental reality, with individuals viewed as products more or less determined by the society in which they live. This view was also carried to extremes by some who postulated an emergent "group mind" to which they seemed to ascribe metaphysically real, if not physically real, existence.

The two extreme views led to major controversy about the "reality" of groups and other collective phenomena, and had the unfortunate historical consequence of widening the communication chasm between sociology and psychology. That chasm is not entirely bridged even today, although the "group mind" controversy has long since been almost forgotten.

A current view of the relation of individual to society, shared by most social psychologists of both psychological and sociological backgrounds, can be summarized as follows. Both individuals and societies are *constructs*, not realities, in a metaphysical sense (just as atoms, molecules, and gravity are only constructs), but both are *real* in the sense that they have observable effects. Furthermore, individuals and societies are *interdependent*. Individual behavior is partly a function of biological and physiological factors, partly a function of social experience. Society is *generated* by interactions and relationships between individuals, but has stability and continuity over time independent of any particular individuals. Society is the *pattern* of its parts, though that pattern is far more complex than a simple summation of properties of the individuals who populate a given society at a given time. We will refer to this issue again when we deal with groups in Part Three.

Early concepts and their current status

Early social philosophers formulated the basic questions of social psychology and provided answers for them. The answers were inadequate in several ways: they were based on limited and crude observations and speculative theory; they tended to be single-factor explanations which tried to account for a wide diversity of phenomena on the basis of a single, simple law or principle; and they tended to be evaluative rather than descriptive. However, these formulations included many fundamental concepts that are still a part of our current theory. Most of these concepts were "discredited" in their original forms, as inadequate one-factor theories of man. They mostly exist today in altered form, embedded in a context of related concepts within a more complex formulation. It is useful to trace some of these transformations so that we can better appreciate the meaning of our present concepts.

HEDONISM: THE PLEASURE/PAIN PRINCIPLE

The Greek hedonists and later the British associationists (James Mill, 1773–1836; Bentham, 1748–1832) formulated the pleasure principle as the fundamental law governing human behavior. This principle states that man always acts so as to maximize the pleasure and minimize the pain or displeasure he receives. As held by the hedonists and as embodied in Bentham's "calculus of pleasure," it assumes that man is aware of all the alternatives available to him in any given choice situation and can estimate the total amount of pleasure and/or pain (including extent, duration, and intensity) each alternative will yield if chosen. It becomes untenable when applied to account for all human behavior.

People obviously make choices (such as committing suicide or performing altruistic acts) which do not appear to maximize pleasure received, at least as viewed by an outside observer. It is possible to argue, of course, that what seems the most pleasurable alternative to one man (the observer) may not be the most pleasurable to another (the actor): one man's "meat" is another man's "poison." Hence, even the man who commits suicide may be choosing the alternative that is most pleasurable or least painful to him as he views the world, even if others do not agree with his view.

Such a broadening of the pleasure principle entirely destroys its usefulness as a scientific "law." This broadened view asserts that in a decision situation men will choose the most pleasurable or least painful alternative, but that there is no basis for predicting just which alternative a given man will choose in a given situation. Whatever alternative he *does* choose is then *presumed* to be the most pleasurable in terms of his own "calculus." This is entirely circular reasoning. It "proves" a principle by a line of reasoning which is based on the assumption that the principle *is* true.

While the pleasure principle failed to work as a *single* principle for explaining human behavior, the basic notion of hedonism still persists in psychology and other fields. For example, Freud's theories use the pleasure principle as a central concept, but in greatly altered form. For Freud, man behaves so as to maximize pleasure, but this has to do with the expression of unconscious instinctual urges, and is not at all a rational or even a conscious "calculation." Unlike the early form of hedonism, Freud's concept of unconscious forces helps to account for man's choices of seemingly unpleasant alternatives. He postulates that the unconscious pleasure-seeking urges become disguised into socially acceptable forms in order to be acted out without recriminations. Hence, what looks like altruistic behavior is merely disguised pleasure seeking. Many current theories of learning give a central place to a derivative of the pleasure principle, namely, the principle that learning is influenced by positive and negative reinforcements.

EGOISM: THE POWER MOTIVE

Egoism is another early concept that was postulated as a principle to explain human behavior. It refers to the premise that man acts as he does in order to attain individual power or aggrandizement and that each man's behavior is determined by his striving for personal power. This point of view accounts nicely for man's aggressive and competitive behavior but encounters difficulty in explaining why man so often exhibits seemingly cooperative behavior. Some proponents of egoism held that society and cooperative behavior exist because of a "social contract" in which men band together in order to protect themselves from a common enemy.

Like hedonism, the power motive was discredited as a single principle for explaining human behavior but it still exists in altered form in current social science theory. While Freud initially made the seeking of pleasure the single primary principle, some of his disciples and some of Freud's own later writings raised the principle of aggression to a place of equal status along with the pleasure principle. Furthermore, a basic substantive question underlying the power principle is still unresolved, namely: Does the process of human development merely cover up more basic human drives with the prohibitions laid down by society? Or does that process produce basic changes in the nature of man's motivation, changing him from an individualistic power seeker to a cooperative social being?

KNOWING, FEELING, AND STRIVING

Plato divided man's behavior into three facets: knowing (the cognitive), feeling (the affective), and striving (the conative). This trilogy of concepts is still used, though often implicitly, as an organizing framework for analysis of human behavior. Furthermore, each of these three facets has been the focus for a historically important theory of behavior.

The principle of *sympathy* gives emphasis to the affective component of behavior as a way of accounting for relationships among people. The concept of sympathy refers to the (pleasurable or painful) feelings a person has in response to the pleasant or unpleasant events that happen to other people. This concept came to have two quite distinct meanings: (1) the more or less automatic reactions of an individual (such as wincing) as he observes the pleasurable or painful experiences of another; and (2) "representational" sympathy, in which the individual imagines the feelings the other must be undergoing. Sympathy, or its absence, was broadened to try to account for all kinds of affect relationships among people as variants of a single principle. Hence it lost its usefulness as a scientific principle.

As an early answer to the key problem of why people within a group behave so much alike, Tarde (1843–1904) formulated the conative principle of *imitation*—that human beings behave as they do because they imitate the behavior of others. Like the concept of sympathy, however, imitation came to include many varieties of behavior: deliberate imitation, unconscious modeling, both reinforced and unreinforced behavior, imitation resulting from identification, and others. Thus, like sympathy, hedonism, and egoism, the single simple principle of imitation was used to explain too much behavioral complexity.

The cognitive principle of *suggestion* arose from the observations and conclusions of the French sociologist Le Bon and earlier hypnotists. Le Bon was concerned with the often violent and abnormal behavior of crowds or mobs. He noted that crowds seem to act with a violence and passion far greater in intensity than would be exhibited by the individuals composing it when acting alone, and that members of a mob seem to experience being "caught up" in the crowd and "losing control" of their own behavior. He also noted, as had many before him, that crowds respond to clever manipulators; hence, they are "suggestible."

The principle of suggestion was used also as the basic explanation of the phenomenon of hypnosis, as represented in the work of Charcot. This work on hypnotism led to Freud's later concepts of unconscious determinants of behavior.

The problem of mob behavior and panics has remained primarily in the field of sociology, and the phenomenon of hypnosis has remained of concern to clinical rather than social psychology. The principle of suggestion, however, is found in current social psychology in the form of concern with interpersonal influence and conformity.

But the concepts of sympathy, imitation, and suggestion are all basically descriptions rather than explanations of phenomena. Thus, when one person behaves according to the expressed wish or command of another person, we can describe, or label, the event as a case of suggestion (or, in more modern terms, as interpersonal influence). Having done so, we do not gain anything by postulating a principle of suggestion as a way of explaining why the event occurred.

Similarly, it does not add to our understanding to try to explain why people act alike by postulating a principle of imitation, which simply asserts that people do act alike. Nor do we increase our understanding of affect relations between people by describing certain relations as sympathy and then explaining why those relations exist between some people and not others by postulating that people differ in tendency for sympathy. In short, when we try to use descriptions as explanations, we are engaging in logically circular reasoning. It was because of this logical circularity, as well as oversimplification, that these early concepts were discredited as explanations of human behavior. However, these concepts, or related ones, still form a part of the much more complex theoretical formulations of present-day social psychology.

INSTINCT, HABIT, AND ATTITUDE AS UNITS OF ANALYSIS

Historically, a number of different concepts have been utilized as basic units of analysis. One early unit of analysis, which was borrowed from the biological sciences by McDougall (1871–1938) and his followers, was the *instinct*. An instinct was thought of as an *innate* predisposition to behave in a certain way. Each human possessed the same basic set of instincts but in differing degrees of intensity. Instincts combined in different ways to form *propensities;* these, in turn, combined to form *sentiments.* Sentiments were persistent ways of orienting toward a given class of objects or ideas.

While McDougall's instinct theory dominated social psychology for many years, it had several basic limitations, which led to its overthrow. First, the instinct theorists could not agree upon what the basic instincts were, or upon procedures by which they could be determined. Consequently, they also could not agree on a list of propensities or sentiments, or on the rules of combination by which these were generated. Far more critical, however, was the instinct theorists' inability to generate convincing evidence for the existence of innate behavior tendencies.

In retrospect, the concept of biologically inherent behavior patterns, borrowed from the study of animals, apparently does not apply to human behavior. In the discussion of heredity versus environment we noted that heredity sets limits while experience channels the actual behavior outcomes. In lower species, some behavior patterns are genetically determined. In man, there may be innate predispositions, but apparently there are no innate behavior patterns as such. While McDougall did not suggest such built-in behavior, many of his critics wrote as if he did.

Even more severe is the criticism that instinct theory is essentially circular: the theorist is free to postulate one or more new instincts as the underlying basis for any particular behavioral phenomenon he wishes to explain. Once again, to account for aggressive behavior by postulating an aggressive instinct does not add to our understanding.

The instinct concept was dethroned as the dominant unit of analysis by the behaviorist concept of the *habit*. A habit was defined as a *learned* stimulus-response cycle, which leads to a fairly automatic form of response when the stimulus conditions associated with it are present. Combinations of learned habits were also used, by Watson (1878–1958), James (1842–1910), and others, to try to account for the more complex forms of human behavior. These attempts to extend the habit concept fell victim to the same problems of oversimplification and circularity that had beset other single-concept explanations. However, the habit, or equivalent concepts, still occupies a central place in learning theory, though within a more comprehensive theoretical structure.

More recently, the central concept of *attitude* has become an important unit of analysis in social psychology. An attitude is a *learned predisposition* to respond positively or negatively to a given class of objects. It thus combines features of both the instinct and habit concepts. Attitudes are distinguished from instincts in that attitudes are learned rather than innate. Attitudes are different from habits in that attitudes are predispositions to feel a certain way toward a class of objects, rather than more or less automatic and fixed responses toward that class of objects. The attitude concept is still very much a part of social psychology, and will be discussed again later.

CHAPTER 3

/ Methods of
social psychology

The logic of research

The general logic of scientific method is the same in all fields of study, but specific techniques vary from one field to another. For example, physics can and does use methods that lead to destruction of the material under study; the human sciences cannot employ such methods. As a new field develops, techniques of study are usually borrowed from related disciplines and adapted to the new area. However, when methods are adapted from one field to another, they often carry with them a type of thinking and some of the concepts of their area of origin, and these are not always appropriate to the new area of application. For example, methods developed for the study of abilities and aptitudes in educational settings (such as achievement testing) are not necessarily adequate for the study of personality or attitudes. Social psychology needs, and is developing, its own methodology.

Scientific method is the systematic observation and recording of behavior, under known conditions, and the application of a rigorous logic to draw conclusions from the recorded results. Features of scientific method include: (1) objectivity of point of view; (2) explicit procedures which can be replicated; (3) reliable measurement under controlled or known conditions; and (4) a sound logic of inference from results to conclusions.

Scientific inquiry asks the following general question: What variables or conditions (X) are related to or associated with differences in a particular phenomenon (Y)? Assume, for example, that you want to know what things are related to or will predict differences in grade-point average of college students (variable Y). Assume, then, that you select a sample of students for study and gather grade-point average information (variable Y) about them. Suppose that you also get a measure of intelligence (variable X_1) and a record of the sex (variable X_2) of each person.

The basic question, then, can be phrased: Do variations in X_1 (I.Q.) correspond to, or covary with, variations in Y (grade-point average)? In other words, are people with high I.Q. scores generally those with high grade-point averages? An alternative form of the question would be: Are differences in X_2 (sex) associated with average differences in Y? That is, do men, on the average, have higher grade-point averages than women, or vice versa?

You must remember, of course, that many other things—family background, motivation, and so forth—may be related to grade-point average. Let us call these factors Z_1, Z_2, etc. The question becomes: What relationship is there between scores on X and Y when other factors that might be related to Y (Z_1, Z_2, etc.) have been taken into account (that is, when these "other factors" are held at a constant value for all cases or balanced within the population being studied)? The question ultimately tested can become very complex, in terms of multiple variables, in terms of the steps needed to control Z's, etc. But the basic question remains: Is Y related to X_1, X_2, etc., as distinct from its relationship to Z_1, Z_2, etc.?

We can describe the logical sequence of research procedure in a general form, although it should be noted that actual research seldom follows this ideal sequence chronologically. First, the scientist notes some phenomenon of interest (Y); in the case of social science, Y is some aspect of human behavior. Then he notes variation in the phenomenon: sometimes Y is present, sometimes not; or sometimes Y exists at a high intensity while it has lower intensity at other times. The scientist then begins a search for concomitants (X's) of the phenomenon Y; that is, he tries to discover conditions (X's) under which Y is or is not present, or conditions (X's) which vary as Y varies. When the scientist has identified an X condition that varies with Y, he then needs to establish whether X causes Y, Y causes X, or X and Y both result from some other phenomenon.

While the general procedure can be stated in a fairly simple form, the research process by which the procedure is carried out is often complicated, requiring elaborate procedures for measuring phenomena (Y's) and associated conditions (X's) and for taking into account the effects of other conditions (Z's). One important requirement for good research is that the study be designed so that the investigator has built-in checks on the inferences he makes from results. We can illustrate some features of good (and poor) research design by the "scotch and soda" story that is often used to satirize the scientific method.

As the story goes, a man we shall call Bill Smith had occasion to drink a lot of scotch and soda one Monday night, and awoke on Tuesday morning with a headache and other symptoms usually termed a hang-over. Being a man who learns from experience, Bill spent Tuesday night drinking bourbon and soda; but alas, on Wednesday morning he had another hang-over. Wednesday night Bill switched to gin and soda, in spite of protests from his drinking companions, but to no avail. He woke up on Thursday with a third hang-over. So our hero, imbued with the spirit of scientific inquiry, reasoned as follows: I want to avoid hang-overs in the future. I have had one each morning for three days. The only common element in the evenings preceding the hang-overs was that I had soda in my drinks on all three occasions. Hence, drinking soda must have caused the hang-overs, and I shall never drink soda again. Furthermore, I shall advise my friends not to do so.

Bill Smith's "research study" illustrates several major types of errors which can, and sometimes do, occur in the design, procedure, and reasoning of actual research studies. First, there is a *logical* error. Soda was not the only common ingredient in Bill's drinks. This error occurred because Bill was making a second methodological error, by looking only at the *superficial properties* of the substances involved. Bourbon is not scotch, by label or other superficial properties, but both have a common property, alcohol, at a more basic or genotypic level.

Bill also made an error in *causal inference* when he reasoned that "soda caused the hang-overs." One cannot legitimately infer that A causes B just because B follows A. Before Bill could legitimately make this inference he would need much more information, including some plausible basis for why the effect occurred—some property of soda capable of producing the observed effects.

Bill's "study" also illustrates several other types of design errors. Before he could really conclude that soda did it, he would have to test a number of other combinations, including: soda only, scotch only, bourbon only, gin only, bourbon and ginger ale, ginger ale only, bourbon and scotch, soda and ginger ale, etc. He would also have to identify conditions under which the phenomenon "hang-over" does *not* occur. To do this, he would have to test what the scientist calls a "control condition," namely, drinking nothing at night. It is conceivable that even if he drank nothing at night Bill would wake up with a headache and other hang-over symptoms because of some physical, psychological, or environmental condition that had nothing at all to do with his evening's activities (such as poor ventilation in his bedroom).

Finally, Bill made an error in generalization when he decided to advise his friends against drinking soda to avoid hang-overs. It is conceivable that Bill did in fact have an adverse reaction to soda, or perhaps to any carbonated beverage, but it does not necessarily follow that other individuals would be similarly affected by that beverage.

While we should not try to make too much out of a facetious example, it may be worth noting that this story has often been used as a humorous argument for the proposition: Scientific reasoning can lead to erroneous conclusions. The preceding discussion should make it amply clear that Bill Smith's "study" actually illustrates a quite different proposition, namely: Erroneous reasoning gives erroneous conclusions, whether it invokes the sacred word "science" or not. We do not make an activity scientific by inserting "therefore" and "whereas" and claiming it is scientific; rather, we make an activity scientific by careful reasoning in our design, procedures, and conclusions.

Settings for the collection of social-psychological data

Social-psychological data can be collected in four major types of settings: surveys, field studies, field experiments, and laboratory studies. These represent different strategies for obtaining information about behavior, and each has different advantages and weaknesses.

SURVEYS

Surveys are studies of the distribution of a particular characteristic in a population (for example, buying habits, voting intentions, responses to civil defense information), or of the relationship between two or more characteristics in a certain population. The characteristic under study and the problem that is of concern together define the population that is relevant. For example, if you want to study voting intentions of women, the relevant population would be females who are eligible to vote. A population may be defined in geographical, occupational, or other terms. Surveys may be conducted on general populations (residents of city X) or on special populations (World War II veterans, subscribers to the *New York Times*).

Generally, the defined population is so large that it is not possible to get data about the characteristics of concern for every member of it. Thus, surveys typically *sample* from the defined population. A sample is drawn by selecting, in some systematic manner, a subset of the members of a defined population, so that data can be gathered for all members of that subset.

The basic form of sampling is *random sampling*. A sample is a random sample if it is drawn by a procedure that *gives each member of the population an equal chance of being included in the sample*. For example, if you wished to study residents of city X and selected a sample from the telephone directory of that city, you would not have a random sample. Residents who do not have phones or have unlisted numbers would have no chance of inclusion in your sample, while others who have both residence and business phone listings would have too high a chance of inclusion. Both of these effects would *bias* your sample if you wanted to generalize results to all residents of the city.

There are many complex forms of sampling which can add power and precision to survey results. For example, you can deliberately oversample a certain kind of case in the population in order to study it more intensively; or you can stratify the population on some characteristic such as age and then sample (randomly) within each age category separately. In *all* cases, *some form of random sampling* is built into the sampling method.

Surveys are often one-time studies of the status of a characteristic (or the existence of a relationship between two characteristics) at a given point in time. Surveys over time can be done, however, in either of two forms: as before-and-after studies of some critical event; or as studies of changes or trends over time. With either of these designs the use of successive samples presents a problem. If new samples are drawn on each occasion, they must be shown to be equivalent in order that the differences over time may be attributed to the critical event or interpreted as changes in time. Use of the same sample a second or third time encounters the problem of attrition (some interviewed the first time are not available the second time) and the more basic problem of whether the people in the first sample have changed because they were interviewed. Resampling the same group is known as the *panel technique*. While some studies have been done to determine the representativeness of panels over time, conclusions are still not definitive. In general, panels can be used at least under some conditions without necessarily biasing results.

Surveys are used to study attitudes, opinions, motivations, expectations of people. They have some inherent problems of methodology regarding sampling, recall of subjects, and deliberate lying by subjects. Further, it is often difficult to validate survey findings against a sample of behavior. Nevertheless, survey methods, which are interdisciplinary in origin but heavily used by social psychologists, are a powerful set of tools for study-

ing behavior. Furthermore, many of the specific techniques used in surveys—interviews, questionnaires, ratings—are used also for measuring
attitudes or behavior within the other three types of data-collection
settings.

FIELD STUDIES

Field studies involve the study of a social phenomenon in its natural
setting. That is, the investigator finds a situation which includes the phenomenon he wishes to study and observes and records the phenomenon
and its surrounding conditions in detail.

For example, Newcomb (1943) studied the attitudes of Bennington
College students toward one another, toward the faculty, and toward a
variety of social and political issues over a period of four years. He found
substantial changes in attitudes from freshman to senior years (in the
direction of more liberal attitudes) and showed that such changes were
related to popularity (generally, the more liberal girls were more popular), attitudes toward the college and its faculty, and changes in attitudes
toward parents. This is an example of a field study, because the investigator did not interfere with an on-going social process (except for the
actual procedures by which he obtained his data) but studied that set
of social phenomena in their natural state.

Field studies permit a thorough account of a given situation. They are
deep, whereas surveys are broad. They may be descriptive (much work
in cultural anthropology is mainly descriptive) or they may be quantitative (that is, they may collect systematic, quantitative data by means of
questionnaires, ratings, and other forms of data collection; Newcomb's
study of Bennington students is an example).

Field studies are usually better suited for exploratory work—that is,
for finding out which are the major variables in a situation and what gross
relationships exist among them—than for definitive testing of precise hypotheses. Field studies are indicated when you know relatively little
about the phenomena to be studied; you must know a lot about a phenomenon to take it into a laboratory setting and study it with precision.

FIELD EXPERIMENTS

Field experiments combine features of the field study and the laboratory experiment. In a field experiment, the investigator studies the phenomenon in a natural or realistic setting but exercises some experimental
control over the main variables he wants to study. For example, Coch and
French (1948) conducted a field experiment in a factory to try to find a
way to prevent decreases in productivity when changes in work procedures are introduced. They set up three conditions: (1) an experimental

condition in which workers helped plan new work methods and participated in setting performance standards for them; (2) an experimental group in which workers participated in planning changes through elected representatives; and (3) a control group in which work changes were instituted by management without prior involvement of the workers. Subsequently, workers in the first experimental condition showed production rate increases (after an initial decrease), while those in the control group showed production rate decreases and did not reattain even their prior levels of productivity. Results for the second condition were intermediate between the first and third conditions. Thus, Coch and French were able to conduct an experiment in which they *created* differences in a key variable (participation by workers in decision) but in which other conditions were left to operate in their natural forms. Thus, field experiments combine some features of the field study and the laboratory experiment.

LABORATORY EXPERIMENTS

In a laboratory experiment the investigator *creates* the situation he wants to study. This is the classical method of the physical sciences. It provides opportunity for control of conditions, for manipulation of the variables of concern, and for precise measurement of the phenomena in question. Results can be attributed as effects of experimental conditions with more assurance than in a field setting because there is more control of other conditions that might be fluctuating in a field setting. However, results may or may not be generalizable to real-life situations, as laboratory conditions are apt to be quite abstract and artificial "representations" of the real-life conditions under which the phenomena occur.

For example, Asch (1956) studied conformity behavior (the tendency for an individual to "give in" to a group) in a laboratory setting. He placed a subject in a room with several other persons, who were presumably also subjects but who were actually working in league with the experimenter. The experimenter asked each subject to judge which of a pair of lines was longer, for a series of pairs of lines. Subjects responded in a fixed order, with the real subject always next to last. On certain trials, by prearrangement, all the pseudosubjects gave the incorrect answer (that is, they judged the shorter of the two lines to be longer). Asch's measure of conformity was the number of times the real subject gave the wrong answer when the confederates did.

This situation offers rigorous control of many conditions—size of "majority," its unanimity, actual length differences in the lines, number of responses of other persons the subject hears before making his own commitment, and so forth. The laboratory situation also permits systematic *manipulation* of many of these variables; in subsequent studies Asch explored the effects on conformity of different-sized majorities, unanimous versus non-unanimous majorities, and other variables.

Asch's results may or may not generalize to conformity in real-life situations, where the effects of many factors not included in the experiments may operate to obscure the conformity effects found in the laboratory. In a sense, the findings of laboratory studies are analogous to the physical science laws about the speed of free-falling bodies in a vacuum. While the law is "true," as stated, it cannot be *directly* applied to predict the speed of bodies falling under real-world conditions, where other variables (such as friction, or air currents) obscure results. Such a law can be used, though, as a base line from which to explore the effects of other variables. This situation also holds for laboratory studies of social psychological phenomena.

Laboratory experiments provide a tool for precise testing of hypotheses. They impose the requirement that you know, or assume you know, quite a bit about the phenomenon in question before you start, in order to be able to create it in the laboratory and to know what conditions need to be controlled.

Laboratory experiments in social psychology pose certain difficulties. Laboratory groups are likely to be artificial, short-lived groups. The situation is less real to the subject than in other types of settings and consequently he may be much less motivated. Further, it is often difficult to make a "strong" manipulation of conditions. (The Asch study is an exception.)

Selection of a data-collection setting is a choice among conflicting goals. The more natural the situation under study, the less control of conditions and the less precision of measurement; therefore, the less certain one can be that results are attributable to any particular variable. Under natural conditions, however, there is apt to be strong subject motivation—the experiment is part of his life, not something he is putting up with temporarily.

On the other hand, the more we go toward the abstract representation of conditions in an artificial laboratory situation, the more we gain precision of measurement and control of variables; but the less subjects are likely to be motivated and the less strong the effects of major variables are likely to be. While one can be more certain that the experimental conditions are the real antecedent conditions for obtained results, it is not always clear to just what range of real-life situations these results can be applied.

There is obviously no one best data-collection setting for all studies.

Each has its strengths and weaknesses, and the choice of setting depends on the purpose of the study. Best of all is programmic research, which uses different types of settings to check and cross check results.

Sources of social-psychological data

Data are records of behavior gathered in a systematic manner. They are usually quantified or categorized in some manner. Some specific aspects are recorded and not others. Thus, *data are coded records of selected aspects of behavior.* In general, social psychology makes use of data from three kinds of sources: observation, self-report, and documents and records.

OBSERVATION

Observation can be done by a human observer or by an instrument. Instruments can record time and can count acts or specific occurrences. A human observer can do these things somewhat less well, but can record also the intensity of various occurrences and the content or meanings of action. However, when you ask human observers to make judgments that require such inferences as intensity or meaning, resulting judgments are apt to be less reliable (that is, less consistent from one observer to another or from one occasion to another) than observations that require only a simple discrimination.

SELF-REPORT

The social sciences have several disadvantages in regard to method compared with the physical sciences. For example, they cannot use methods that might destroy or injure their objects of study (human beings). On the other hand, they have one major advantage: they can obtain data about conditions as they are experienced by the subjects. Various kinds of data obtained from verbal reports of subjects are here grouped as self-report data.

Self-report data can be accumulated in either of two general forms: interview or questionnaire. Interviews are face-to-face situations in which the interviewer records the verbal responses of the interviewee, and perhaps notes nonverbal aspects of the subject's behavior. Questionnaires are forms that ask the respondent certain questions, and the respondent records his own answers.

Both interviews and questionnaires vary in the degree to which the questions and the forms of answers are structured in advance. A relatively structured interview would be one that poses a series of predetermined questions, asked verbatim, and that provides only limited categories of response. (A lawyer's questioning of a witness in court, in the "answer yes or no" fashion, would be an example of a structured interview.) Semistructured interviews provide a general set of questions with verbatim recording of the subject's response (for example, an oral exam). Even more unstructured would be an interview in which only the general topics to be covered are fixed in advance, and the interviewer follows up answers to general questions with specific "probes" (a medical diagnostic interview would be an example). Projective tests, which present the subject with an almost totally ambiguous stimulus (such as the Rorschach "inkblot" test) and ask him to respond with whatever the stimulus brings to mind, are examples of very unstructured interviews.

The same continuum of structured-unstructured applies to questionnaires, which can use fixed questions with fixed-answer alternatives (for example, a true-false exam), fixed questions with open-end "free" response (for example, an essay exam), or general questions with open-end or free-response answers. Projective tests have also been used in questionnaire form.

Data obtained by use of the more structured types of questions vary also in their metric properties (measurement form). The main ones for consideration here are ratings, rankings, and choice behavior.

Ratings are judgments that a certain object (person, idea, thing) has a *certain amount* of a given characteristic. The characteristic may be specific or general. An example of a general characteristic would be a rating of the "leadership ability" of a particular person, perhaps in terms of a 10-point scale whose end points are defined as "very outstanding" and "very poor."

Rankings are *comparative* judgments about a set of objects (persons, ideas, things) with regard to a given characteristic. Again, the characteristic on which the objects are to be ranked may be specific or general. For example, we might ask each member of a group to rank all members of the group in terms of how well he, the ranker, likes them, giving the most liked person rank 1, the second most liked rank 2, and so on.

Choice behavior ("Check all the members of the group whom you like") is a special case of ratings. Such a choice question is equivalent to asking: "Indicate which members of the group—any, all, or none—meet your standard for a likeable person."

Ratings and rankings have complementary advantages and disadvantages. For ratings, one major disadvantage is that raters (at least in our culture) tend to give favorable ratings of most people. Thus, resulting data often do not permit differentiations to be made among the persons being rated. A major disadvantage of rankings is that there is no way to anchor them as to magnitude on the characteristic in question. For example, we do not know whether the person getting the highest ranking on leadership in a given group is a good, mediocre, or poor leader; we only know that he is better than the others in that particular group. The opposite is also true regarding the lower-ranked members; a man could be the poorest leader in a given group but still a very good leader.

Ratings are strong where rankings are weak and vice versa. Ratings anchor the responses to amount of the characteristic, while rankings guard against the tendency to give all favorable ratings. Each technique is useful for different purposes, and must be interpreted in its own terms.

DOCUMENTS AND RECORDS

Records refer to systematically coded, usually quantified, descriptions of events (the number of Navy recruits from Cook County in June 1956; the number of persons entering mental hospitals at age 30 or higher). Documents usually refer to verbal descriptive records, such as diaries, newspaper reports, books, official papers, and speeches. Records and documents are essentially data in a frozen form. They may represent someone's observations of behavior or events, or they may represent self-report data by someone about his own feelings, attitudes, or perceptions of events. Documents and records have the same kinds of advantages and disadvantages as self-report and observation data. They have the additional advantage of being permanent or stable in time. However, they have the additional disadvantage of being data that were collected according to someone else's plan. Therefore they may or may not provide information to test the questions you want to investigate. If documents do not already exist in coded and quantified form, the data must be categorized before they can be used in statistical tests. The process of categorizing or coding verbal material (spoken or written) is referred to as content analysis. Content analysis is a major technique in some of the social sciences such as journalism and political analyses.

Analysis of data: From data to conclusions

Social psychologists make much use of statistics for analysis of data, so a word is in order about what statistics are and what they can and cannot do. Statistics can do two things. First, statistics can be used to help summarize a mass of raw data into a simplified, comprehensible picture. Statistics serve as a summarizing tool, for example, when a student cites his over-all grade-point average rather than his individual grades in each of many courses, or when a baseball player's batting average is quoted rather than the outcome of his every time at bat.

Statistics are used also as a tool for assessing how probable or improbable a given set of events is. For example, we know intuitively that the chance of flipping heads on a coin is 1 in 2; the chance of drawing a king of spades from a normal deck of cards is 1 in 52. The odds on getting a perfect bridge hand are not as intuitively obvious, but can be calculated. All these calculations are predicated on the assumption that the coin flip, card draw, or card deal are determined by *chance factors only;* that is, that the coin is not loaded and the cards are not stacked.

If someone flipped many heads in a row or drew the same card on each of several dozen draws, we would begin to be suspicious of the assumption that only chance factors were operating. More specifically, we would generate the hypothesis that some kind of biasing factor(s) was operating. If the disproportion continued long enough—that is, if the *obtained results* got further and further from what we would reasonably expect if only chance were operating—we would eventually *conclude* that some nonchance factor(s) was involved.

But why should anyone be concerned with chance results? Suppose, for example, that you want to test the hypothesis that an experimental group which received a certain treatment (X_1) will have higher scores on some test (Y) than a control group which received a different treatment (X_2). You must design the study, of course, so that alternative hypotheses (about other factors, Z_1, Z_2, etc.) cannot account for obtained differences in Y. If you do not do this, you will not be able to attribute differences in Y to the effects of your experimental treatment. One major alternative hypothesis that is always present is the *chance hypothesis;* that is, that the obtained differences between groups X_1 and X_2 in their scores on Y could easily have occurred on a chance basis, and hence were not produced by the experimental treatment. It is only when you have some basis for *rejecting* the chance hypothesis (often called the "null hypothesis"), because the odds are very small (say 99 to 1) that obtained results could have occurred by chance, that you have any basis for concluding that your experimental treatment had the intended effect.

The assessing function of statistics involves various procedures for estimating the odds that a given set of results would occur if only chance were operating. For example, if you obtain results that would only occur by chance 1 time in 100, the odds are 99 to 1 that they are not entirely chance results. We might then reasonably conclude that the results are non-chance, and we would *know the degree of confidence* (99 to 1) *which we can place in that conclusion.* Thus, the main function that statistics serves for social science is to provide an *explicit and replicable logic by which we can assess the likelihood that chance alone accounts for our data.* Statistical operations do not add anything to the data; they merely give us a systematic basis on which to draw and communicate our conclusions, and a built-in estimate of the probability that our conclusions (about the chance hypothesis) are in error.

Thus, analysis of social science data is basically a comparison of results against the probability that such results would occur by chance. In general, statistical tests are tests of the null hypothesis; that is, they test the hypothesis that obtained results are not significantly different from what could have occurred by chance. When the odds that the results occurred by chance are as low as 1 in 20, or 1 in 100, the results are said to be "statistically significant." When this occurs, the scientist may reject the null hypothesis and consider his own hypothesis supported. That is, he may conclude that his results cannot reasonably be attributed to chance. If other aspects of his design are sound, he may further presume that obtained results occurred because of the effects of the conditions which he is studying.

The amount of a difference required to be significant (not likely to be due to chance) depends on the number of cases being studied. The more cases, the more stable the findings, and thus the less the difference needed for a nonchance difference. For example, if you flip 10 coins, it would not be surprising to get 6 heads and 4 tails, a 60 percent to 40 percent split. If you flip 10,000 coins, however, it would be highly unlikely that you would get as great a disproportion of heads and tails as 60 percent and 40 percent. Almost certainly the coins would split much nearer to 50–50 (provided only chance factors were operating).

At a gross level, statistical tests can be considered as of two types: tests of differences (for example, differences between the average scores of two groups, say of an experimental and a control group); and tests of association or covariation (for example, association between two variables such as age and I.Q. score). There are many statistical tests of both types, and they vary in their applicability. For example, some statistical tests permit the use of qualitative data (observations classified into two or more categories), while other statistical tests require that the data be in the form of quantitative scores. As with the choice of data source and form, and of data collection settings, there is no one best statistical test. Choice of the statistic to use in a given case depends on the specific question to be answered and on the form of the data.

Methods selected throughout the research process affect results, because the specific data-collection or data-analysis method used affects the specific questions that can be answered from the data. Choices of methods depend on what is already known about the phenomena under study. The more that is known, the more powerful the methods that can be applied and the more efficiently they can be applied; thus, the more precise the new information that can be gained.

SUPPLEMENTARY READING

History of Social Psychology

Allport, G. W. The historical background of modern social psychology. In G. Lindzey (Ed.), *Handbook of social psychology.* Reading, Mass.: Addison-Wesley Publishing Company, Inc., 1954. Chap. 1.

Cartwright, D., & Zander, A. *Group dynamics, research and theory.* New York: Harper & Row, Publishers, 1960. Chaps. 1 and 2.

Methods of Social Psychology

Festinger, L., & Katz, D. *Research methods in the behavioral sciences.* New York: Holt, Rinehart and Winston, Inc., 1953.

Heyns, R. W., & Lippitt, R. Systematic observational techniques. In G. Lindzey (Ed.), *Handbook of social psychology.* Reading, Mass.: Addison-Wesley Publishing Company, Inc., 1954. Chap. 10.

Selltiz, C., Jahoda, M., Deutsch, M., & Cook, S. W. *Research methods in social relations.* New York: Holt, Rinehart and Winston, Inc., 1962.

PART TWO /

The Individual

The social basis of humanness

The newborn infant comes into the world equipped with certain basic, biologically determined drives (such as hunger and thirst); with certain capacities to be stimulated (by touch, light, sound); and with certain capacities to respond (with gross sound, movements), mostly in a random manner.

This relatively undifferentiated organism becomes a human child, and then a human adult, through the process of learning. Learning occurs through systematic associations of different stimulus patterns one with another and through selective reinforcement (reward and punishment) of certain responses.

37

The "significant others" in the child's world, persons with whom he is closely associated, most notably the mother or someone acting in her place, are crucial for that learning in several respects:

1. They administer rewards and punishments. Rewards are satisfactions of the child's needs and wants; punishments are frustrations or non-satisfactions of these needs and wants.
2. They do so selectively.
3. They vary in *how* they reward and punish, that is, which stimulus-response patterns they reward, which they punish, and the manner in which they carry out those reinforcements.

The "significant others" in a given child's environment are not all alike, nor do they all act alike toward the child. The particular relationship parents establish with a child results in part from the past learning, the culture, of the parents. Thus, the process of learning by which an infant becomes a human child is largely determined by the social environment of the child. It is eminently a social process.

This does not imply that genetic or biological factors are of no consequence. The individual's native physical and intellectual capacities operate as *upper limits* on the characteristics that he is capable of learning. For example, it is probable that the upper limit of an individual's *basic* intelligence is determined genetically, in large part; his maximum rate of learning may also depend on hereditary factors. But the actual level of attainment *exhibited* by the child or the adult is highly contingent on features of his social environment. Both the extent and the directions in which the individual learns depend on the social, interactive, reward-and-punishment situation that he experiences in the child-parent relationship (and in other later interpersonal relationships). There is evidence, for example, that the extent and form of aggression, the adequacy of sexual adjustment and of adjustment to adult responsibilities, and the general adaptive behavior of the organism are all influenced by the social environment in which the individual lives.

The social environment cannot "make a silk purse out of a sow's ear." Neither can heredity make a highly adaptive, intelligent organism, independent of the social environment of that organism. Helen Keller's life illustrates this point well. As a blind, deaf, and apparently mute child, she was considered to be mentally defective and acted in a very primitive, unsocialized way. However, once she had been taught to communicate effectively with her environment (first by sign language and later by speech), she proved to be not only adequate but quite outstanding, intellectually and in other ways.

Thus "people make people out of people." Socialization, the social learning process by which the infant becomes "humanized," and humanized in a particular way, depends on an *interaction* of biological and social-environmental factors. One of the products of that socialization process is the development of what is termed "individual personality."

CHAPTER 4

Learning motives and attitudes

For purposes of this book, we will use the following definitions of basic terms. Other writers use and define some of these terms differently. These definitions generally follow Newcomb's (1950) usage.

A *drive* is organized or focused energy. In general, this term will be used in relation to basic physiological states of an organism, such as hunger, thirst, and the need for air. Drives occur periodically (for example, hunger recurs every few hours in an infant) as a direct consequence of the organism's physiological processes.

A *motive* is a drive to which a goal has become "connected." For example, when we as adults say we are hungry, we imply that we need or want to consume food. Motives represent the systematic connection of a particular response or set of responses (eating) with a particular drive state (hunger). Whereas basic drives are innate, motives are learned.

An *attitude* is an orientation toward (a way of believing and feeling about) an object or class of objects. Attitudes are learned. They may be general or specific. They represent *predispositions* to respond, favorably or unfavorably, toward the "target" of the attitude, but are not overt responses as such.

Personality refers to the total organization of the individual's motives, attitudes, beliefs, ways of perceiving, and ways of behaving. Personality does not mean "sociability," not something individuals have more or less of. Nor is it a matter of good or bad. We can speak of well-adjusted or poorly adjusted individuals, but only meaningfully in the context of some social setting.

Newcomb (1950) defines personality as: "The individual's organization of predispositions to behavior." He states that personality is: (1) *unique* to each individual (although with lots of similarity for persons with similar social environment); (2) *persistent* (it changes, but slowly); (3) *dynamic* (it is the orientation of the person to the environment); (4) *social* (it is influenced by social interaction in its development and in its changes); and (5) *organized*.

The social learning process

For present purposes, we will talk about two kinds of learning: instrumental learning and associative learning. Assume that we have an organism which is capable of being stimulated by (will respond to) a certain event or stimulus, S_1. When S_1 occurs, the organism produces a more or less random series of responses, R_a, R_b, R_c, etc. If we always *reward* R_b (for example, if S_1 is a hunger state and we always give food when the organism produces response R_b), then the sequence: S_1——R_b will come to occur systematically. That is, when S_1 occurs, R_b will occur at a high level of probability. We will call this kind of connection *instrumental learning*. The response, R_b, becomes "connected" with S_1 as a means for obtaining a desirable state (reduction of hunger).

If we present S_2 along with S_1 a number of times, the response R_b will occur as before. If we then present S_2 *without* S_1, response R_b will continue to occur, because it has become associated with S_2 as well as with S_1. This form of connection will be called *associative learning*. The connection of S_2 with R_b develops because S_2 was associated with S_1 in time and space.

Both instrumental and associative learning take place in the early development of the child. The initial responses of the newborn infant to the pangs of hunger, thirst, or bodily discomforts are essentially random emissions of the only responses of which he is capable: noise and random movement. If an adult feeds the infant, thus satisfying the hunger drive, the responses involved in the consummatory act (sucking, swallowing) and those involved in "signaling" the need (such as crying) become connected with the internal stimulus (drive state) of hunger. This illustrates instrumental learning and the learning of a motive.

At the same time, if a stimulus pattern ("mother") is consistently associated with the feeding situation, even though not *intrinsically* related to the internal drive state (hunger) or to its satisfaction (by ingestion of food), that stimulus pattern will also become connected with (and will call out the same feelings as) the drive-satisfaction sequence with which it is associated. This illustrates associative learning and the learning of an attitude (that is, a favorable or unfavorable predisposition to respond toward the stimulus, mother).

The development of human nature can be viewed as a proliferation of learned stimulus-response patterns, of both instrumental and associational types, into more and more complex, organized patterns of motives, attitudes, and behavior. The total organization of the individual's motives, attitudes, and behaviors is termed the "personality" of the individual.

Motives and attitudes

Attitudes refer to cognitive and affective states of the organism. Motives refer to the dynamic or energizing components of behavior. Motives are drives that have associated goals. They operate intermittently. Attitudes are predispositions toward objects. They exist continuously. Both of these concepts are intervening variables; that is, they are not directly observable, but rather are *inferred* from stimulus-response consistencies.

Attitudes are learned orientations toward objects, or predispositions to behave in certain ways toward a given object or class of objects. An attitude always has an object (person, thing, concept), and it always has a sign (positive or negative). Attitudes may be general or specific. They vary in intensity and in direction (positive or negative). Attitudes do not exist in isolation. They are related to one another in an over-all attitudinal structure. Attitudes develop in the service of motives and are part of the behavior patterns by which drive satisfactions are obtained.

Motives in the first instance are learned responses to basic needs of the organism—hunger, thirst, breathing. Survival depends on satisfactions of these needs, and the cooperation of other adult human beings is essential to their satisfaction. Thus, motives are learned in the context of interpersonal interaction.

Satisfaction of basic drives gives the child security, while frustration of these drives arouses anxiety. The context surrounding arousal and satisfaction of a drive can itself become a rewarding or a punishing situation (associative learning). Thus, the mother-child relationship during feeding can take on secondary reinforcement value by threatening or enhancing security. This interpersonal relationship usually generalizes (by associative learning) to other interactions with the mother and to interactions with other persons. Such secondary motives can be thought of as becoming *functionally autonomous;* that is, interactions which lead to an increase of security or reduction of threat become *satisfying in their own right.*

Motive blocking, anxiety, and conflict

Behavior patterns associated with drive satisfaction are learned. If a behavior pattern fails to satisfy the motive on which it is based (for example, because the environment has changed), new behavior patterns have to be formed. Although new behavior patterns may be discovered by random, exploratory behavior, they are most likely to be tried when old patterns are blocked. Thus, motive blocking helps develop personality.

Motive blocking may lead to adaptive or problem-solving behavior: development of new paths to the goal, removal of obstacles, substitution of a new goal. On the other hand, motive blocking may lead to threat-oriented rather than problem-solving behavior. Threat-oriented behavior is action to protect one's own security rather than to remove or circumvent the obstacle to motive satisfaction. Examples include retreat or withdrawal; aggression (often against a substitute, or inward against oneself); and regression to forms of behavior characteristic of earlier levels of development.

When motive blocking is viewed as threatening, anxiety is aroused. It is important to distinguish between fear and anxiety. Fear is related to a real and present danger, whereas anxiety refers to an uncertain, nonspecific danger. Anxiety is usually disproportionate to the "danger" as viewed objectively. While a motive can be described as an organization of energy to be expended in seeking a certain goal, anxiety is an organization of energy to *avoid* certain actions or states of affairs.

Conflict refers to *self blocking* of a motive. It is a special case of motive blocking, and all the types of responses described above apply. Three types of conflict can be distinguished: (1) approach/approach conflicts, or choices between two attractive alternatives; (2) threat/threat conflicts, or choices between two threatening alternatives; and (3) appeal-with-threat conflicts, or choices between two or more alternatives, each of which is both appealing and threatening. Conflicts (especially the second and third types above) also can lead to the arousal of anxiety and to the learning of new behavior patterns. Problem solving under conditions of high anxiety is not always productive. Yet some degree of motive blocking and conflict, with associated anxiety, seems to be a necessary condition for human development.

CHAPTER 5

/ *Social factors in perception*

In Chapter 4 we described the development of personality as a social learning process in which the individual's interaction with others leads to the development and organization of motives, attitudes, and patterns of behavior. One important part of the development of personality is the process of perception, by which the individual gains "knowledge" about his environment. Perception refers to the link between the actual reception of energy through the sense organs, which is called *sensation,* and such mental processes as judgment, reasoning, and memory. That is, perception has to do with the translation of raw energy "data" into meaningful experience.

Human perception is a complicated set of phenomena, one that has become a major field of specialization within psychology. What a given individual will perceive in a given stimulus situation depends on many physiological and psychological factors such as sensory acuity, learning rates, and prior learning levels, as well as on properties of the stimulus patterns which are the objects of perception. We cannot begin to cover adequately even the major phenomena from this field of study in the space that we can devote to the topic of perception, so we shall limit our discussion of perception to those aspects that have to do with the influence of social factors.

The first point to be made is that perception is an active process. That is, human beings *put meaning* into stimulus patterns; they do not just "recognize" meanings which are inherent in those stimuli. Furthermore, we are prone to perceive what we *expect* and to fail to perceive things that do not fit our expectations. In fact, under some conditions, we perceive what we *want* to perceive, not necessarily what is actually present in the stimulus pattern. The extent to which factors in the perceiver—his expectations, motives, attitudes—affect perception depends on how strong those factors are and how strong or compelling the stimulus pattern is. The more clear-cut or structured the stimulus pattern, the less it is amenable to perceptual distortion. Conversely, the more ambiguous the stimulus pattern, the more leeway there is for factors in the perceiver to operate in determining what is perceived.

In this chapter we will examine three major questions. First, we will consider how language, through which man gains so much of his knowledge about the world, influences what the individual perceives. Then we will consider how the operation of certain motives and attitudes affects what is perceived. Finally, we will discuss some features of one special kind of perception, namely, the perception of other people.

Language and perception

One important part of the socialization process is the development of language. A language is a set of symbols that stand for "things" (objects, ideas, and so on). Symbols of language do not have *intrinsic* meaning; they come to have meanings by a process of social consensus. The letters *h, o, r, s,* and *e,* written together, "mean" to us a certain type of four-legged mammal, *because we have arbitrarily agreed* that this set of graphic symbols will have that meaning. For another group of people, those who use the German language, the letters *P, f, e, r,* and *d* are used to designate that same animal species, because of a similar social consensus. These are arbitrary mappings of symbols to "things," established by social consensus.

The child learns the language of those who socialize him as a part of the learning process previously described. The words of others are stimuli that come to have meaning because they occur in association with rewarding or punishing circumstances. The utterances of the child are responses which become learned because they help (or hinder) his attempts to get what he wants.

A language provides a classification of "things"—objects, events, and experiences. Thus, our language is the basis for our "reality." If a language uses a single word to denote a certain set of objects, then those objects *are alike* for the people who use that language. If a different language has one word for a certain subset of those objects and a different word for another subset, then the whole set of objects contains two kinds of things for persons who use that language. The "beliefs" or "perceptions" about reality are different for these two groups.

For example, our language has only one word for snow in all its forms. The Eskimos use a language that has a number of words to distinguish between snow in different forms or conditions: snow falling, snow on the ground, snow used for building a dwelling. Conversely, a number of languages probably do not yet contain many of the fine distinctions we make in areas of our industrial technology. It is doubtful, for example, if a person raised in one of the cultures of the South Pacific would understand the distinction we make between chemists, chemical engineers, fuel technologists, and physical chemists; or between psychiatrists, psychoanalysts, and psychologists.

Thus, the language we use determines what similarities and differences we are *equipped to perceive* in the world around us. Language is learned. Hence, our perceptions of the world and our beliefs about it are also learned, as a part of the socialization process.

Effects of motives and attitudes on perception

Motives, attitudes, and perceptions are all interrelated as a part of the individual's over-all personality organization. It has already been noted that attitudes arise and function in the service of motives. The perceptual process, likewise, operates to aid the satisfaction of man's needs. For example, if we are walking down an unfamiliar city street, we might or might not notice any of a variety of buildings, business establishments, signs, benches, and other objects, or the people who are on the street. We could easily walk several blocks and not know whether we had passed a mailbox, or a restaurant, or a bus stop. If we had decided to eat lunch, however, it is likely that we would notice every restaurant along the street. Similarly, if we had a letter to mail, or wanted to ride a bus, we would probably notice a mailbox, or a bus-stop sign, if one were present. This would occur, of course, because under the latter conditions we are attending to and actively searching for particular stimulus patterns, while we are "not paying any attention" to those stimuli under the former conditions. In other words, we never perceive *all* that is "out there," all the stimuli that are actually impinging on our sense organs. We perceive *selectively*, and the selection is related to what we care about.

This same point has been demonstrated in research studies done with far more rigor than the examples given here. For example, Levine, Chein, and Murphy (1942) studied the perceptions of subjects who had not eaten for many hours. Subjects were asked to identify objects in a set of pictures which were presented behind a ground-glass screen that obscured them to the point of ambiguity. As the number of hours of food deprivation increased, subjects were able to "detect" food and food-related objects (such as knives and forks) more and more, up to about twelve hours of starvation. After that the number of food associations decreased.

In another study, McClelland and Atkinson (1948) found that hungry subjects "saw" more food-related objects (but not food as such) even when *no* stimulus pattern was projected on the viewing screen. Just as we search for mailbox or restaurant, these subjects were searching (although unconsciously) for objects related to a strongly aroused motive.

Perception is also affected by persistent attitudes as well as by momentarily strong motive states. Bruner and Goodman (1947) asked children to match a spot of light to the size of several different coins by manipulating a knob that would vary the size of the light. The children tended to overestimate the size of all coins. Poorer children, however, overestimated much more than did children of wealthy families, especially for coins of larger denomination. Presumably, the poorer children had more intense positive attitudes toward money; it was literally more valuable to them than to the wealthier children. Neither rich nor poor children overestimated size when asked to match the spot of light to paper discs of various sizes.

Thus our motives, our attitudes, and even our "social position" as reflected in family wealth, all can affect what we see in the world around us. Note that in two of these stimulus situations there really was an underlying "true stimulus pattern": the set of pictures projected on the screen and the actual coins. Many of the judgments we make in our day-to-day lives do not have any underlying "true stimulus." For such matters, where there is no "physical reality," we tend to develop a "social reality" around which to organize our perceptions. Such perceptions are highly influenced by the motives and attitudes of the perceiver. Thus, since motives and attitudes are learned in the course of the socialization process, human perception of both physical and social "facts" is based on a social, interactive process.

The perception of other people

Oliver Wendell Holmes (1809–1894) once described a famous conversation between John and Henry in which six "persons" took part: John, as John knew himself; John, as he was known to Henry; the "true" John, as he was known only to God; and the equivalent trio of Henrys.

This same basic insight into the special nature of interpersonal perception was reflected in the work of early sociologists, notably in Cooley's (1902) concept of the "looking-glass self" and in George Mead's (1934) concepts of the two selves, the "I" and the "me." Both men pointed out that the child first develops an awareness of himself as an entity separate and distinct from his environment because *other people* respond to him as a separate, autonomous object. If there were no other people, we would have no self concept. As an individual develops a concept of "self," he becomes aware of himself as an object of his own perception (Mead's "me"), as distinct from himself as the perceiver (Mead's "I"). Furthermore, his own evaluation of himself arises as a *reflection of others' evaluation of him*. Thus, argued Mead and Cooley, the very heart of the individual's personality, his own self concept, arises in the first instance and develops through time by the process of social interaction with other people.

Since these early formulations, there has been much research and theory on the nature and consequences of interpersonal perceptions. One whole school of psychotherapy (see Rogers, 1942) is built upon Mead's premise that the self concept is crucial to adjustment and that self evaluation changes in response to changes in others' evaluations of oneself. On this premise, the crux of therapy is to provide the patient with a consistently warm and accepting social environment, thus providing a proper climate for him to reorient his self concept. Recently, Fiedler and his coworkers (1959) have shown that interpersonal perceptions are related to the individual's adjustment. In a large study of both military and college living groups, they found that individuals who see themselves as similar to others with whom they have close associations and who are seen as similar by those "significant others" show better personal adjustment than persons for whom this is not the case.

Newcomb (1953) points out that our perceptions of other people are closely tied to our attitudes on matters related to those people. We tend to agree with those we like and like those with whom we agree. We also tend to disagree with those we dislike and dislike those with whom we disagree. Newcomb has formalized these ideas in a theoretical model that summarizes many of the concepts in this area. Newcomb's model deals with two persons (*A* and *B*) engaged in interaction about one or more objects (*X*'s), which can be ideas, physical objects, or other people. The set of attitudes which *A* and *B* have about each other and about the *X*'s constitutes a system of interrelated parts. This set of attitudes is a system because the parts are interdependent, and when one part changes other parts are likely to show compensating changes. In fact, Newcomb postulates that there are certain states of the system (patterns of attitudes) which constitute *balanced* or *equilibrium* states. These balanced states are: mutual attraction between *A* and *B*, along with agreement about *X*'s; and mutual rejection between *A* and *B* along with disagreement about *X*'s. All other states (such as disagreement with mutual attraction) are unstable states and will tend toward one or another of the equilibrium patterns.

The Objective System

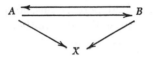

A's attitudes toward *B* and *X*
and *B*'s attitudes toward *A* and *X*

The Subjective Systems

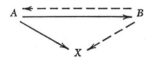 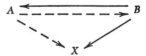

From *A*'s point of view   From *B*'s point of view

A's attitudes toward *B* and *X*   B's attitudes toward *A* and *X*
and *A*'s perceptions (estimates)   and *B*'s perceptions (estimates)
of *B*'s attitudes toward *A* and *X*   of *A*'s attitudes toward *B* and *X*

FIGURE 1 Diagram of Newcomb's *A-B-X* Model of Systems of Interpersonal Relationships. *A* and *B* represent two persons; *X* represents an object about which *A* and *B* are communicating or toward which *A* and *B* are co-orienting. Solid arrows represent actual attitudes of one person toward the other or toward *X*. Arrows run from holder of the attitude to target of the attitude. Broken-line arrows represent estimates by one person of the other person's attitudes; for example, *B* — — — — — → *X* represents *A*'s estimate of *B*'s attitude toward *X*.

Underlying this "objective" system or pattern of attitudes are two "subjective" A-B-X systems, one for A and one for B. A's subjective system includes his attitudes toward B and toward X and his *perceptions* (estimates) of B's attitudes toward himself (A) and toward X. B's subjective system includes the corresponding attitudes and perceptions. The same kinds of balanced states (perceived agreement with positively attractive others, and perceived disagreement with negatively attractive others) and the same tendency toward system balance hold for the subjective systems as for the objective A-B-X system. These systems of interpersonal relationships are shown in Figure 1.

Thus, Newcomb is saying that the famous John and Henry conversation includes two other "persons" besides the six listed by Holmes, namely: John as John believes Henry sees him; and Henry's perception of how John sees Henry. Newcomb is also postulating that these interpersonal perceptions are interdependent with John's and Henry's own attitudes about the topics of their interaction and with their perceptions of each other's attitudes. Thus, at a more general level, he postulates that interpersonal attitudes, interpersonal perceptions, and attitudes toward other objects are all interdependent with one another, tend to be compatible, and tend to change together as a system.

CHAPTER 6

/ *Human personality*

Less than a century ago, Sigmund Freud, a student of the French psychiatrist Charcot, began to study patients who showed physical symptoms without apparent physical cause, and patients who suffered extreme mental distress but did not show any physical symptoms. Freud concluded that these disorders had psychological rather than organic (physical) causes. Many years of collecting clinical evidence about these disorders and their causes led Freud to a definitive theoretical view of human behavior, which is now called psychoanalysis.

Psychoanalysis is both a theory of personality and a method for the treatment of certain kinds of psychological disorders. We shall be concerned primarily with the former. (For a more complete presentation of Freudian theory, see Hall & Lindzey, 1957, Chap. 2.) Freud's concepts literally revolutionized clinical and social psychology and a number of related fields. While many would take issue with Freud's theory today, no one would dispute his total impact on the field. He generated a totally new way of looking at human behavior, and most work done since his time has reflected his concepts, at least in part.

Basic concepts of Freudian personality theory

Freud's basic concept is that personality disorders and intraindividual conflict arise because man's biological drives are inevitably in conflict with the restraints society imposes on the individual. The main biological (instinctive) drive he terms *libido* or *sex drive*.[1]

The sum total of all instinctual drives is termed the *id*. The id comes into conflict with society, and out of this conflict there evolves a second part of the personality, the *ego*. The ego mediates between the organism (its id) and reality. In time, the individual incorporates within himself the standards of society—as laid down by his parents and other significant persons in his childhood environment—and these standards become a third force within the individual, termed the *superego*.

The psychological adjustment of the individual depends upon how well the ego can manage to deal with the demands of the id and the conflicting demands of the superego, giving each its proper degree of influence but neither its complete head, and at the same time keep the organism in a reasonable relationship with external reality. Failure of the ego to maintain this complex balance produces personality maladjustments of various forms.

Freud also established the basic concept of the unconscious. For Freud, many of the forces that affect our behavior operate at deeper levels of the personality, and we are not consciously aware of them. As the organism develops, conflict necessarily occurs between the basic, instinctual drives of the id and the constraints of society (in reality, and as incorporated into the superego). When such conflict occurs, and when direct expression of libidinal impulses is therefore blocked, the organism is apt to *repress* the impulse to the unconscious levels of the personality. That impulse is not lost, however, nor is it divested of the energy (drive) toward its expression. Rather, the impulse becomes modified by one or another mechanism into a form that will permit a substitute or disguised expression of the original impulse in socially accepted behavior. Such "mechanisms" for substitute gratification of the id include rationalization (unconscious development of a socially "good" reason for behavior in the service of the socially unacceptable motive), projection (attributing one's own unacceptable motivations to someone else), and so on.

[1] While Freud treated sex as the single basic drive (our old friend the pleasure principle), later followers and some of Freud's later work elevated aggression (our old friend egoism) to an equally primary place (see Chapter 2).

One means for disguised expression of unacceptable impulses is through dreams. Freud held that dreams are the expression of blocked (repressed) libidinous impulses in symbolized and disguised form. He used the analysis of dreams as a tool for diagnosis of the individual. Psychoanalysis as a method of treatment is a one-step derivative of the dream-analysis method. Freud also analyzed many everyday behaviors (such as slips of the tongue, humor) in terms of their function in expressing repressed libidinous impulses.

Freud's view of personality development

Initially, the child's main contact with the world is by mouth, and libidinous pleasure is obtained through sucking. The oral zone is the focus of such erogenous pleasure. The child's main interaction is with the mother in the feeding situation. A satisfying relationship here develops security. An unsatisfying relationship may lead to a fixation on oral incorporative (sucking) behavior or on oral aggressive (biting) behavior. Such a fixation at the oral stage may lead to the development of a personality whose main modality for substitute gratification of repressed libidinous impulses later in life is oral. That is, he may tend to "regress" back to behavior characteristic, or symbolic, of the oral stage. Freud and his followers interpret behaviors such as smoking, nail biting, verbal sarcasm, and compulsive eating or drinking as forms of regression to the oral stage.

As maturation continues, about age 1 or 2, the anal zone becomes the focus of erogenous impulses, and the eliminatory functions become central to the parent-child interaction. Toilet-training interaction can lead to anal compulsive (hold back) or anal expulsive (let go) types of overreaction. Unsatisfactory experience here can lead to fixation at this stage. For example, Freud considered overfastidiousness, petty discipline, and hoarding behavior as characteristic of anal personality types.

Then, somewhere between age 2 and 5, the genital zone becomes the focus of erogenous impulses. Autoeroticism (masturbation or stimulation of genitals) becomes the primary source of libidinous satisfaction. Freud calls this the phallic stage. It coincides with the period of time of the Oedipus complex.

The Oedipus complex refers to a libidinous attraction of the male child to his mother, accompanied by fear and rivalry toward his father. (The Electra complex is Freud's term for the female equivalent.) When the society blocks the libidinous satisfactions of autoerotic behavior and/or the impulses associated with the Oedipus complex, as is often the case in our society, the individual may become fixated at the genital stage. A latency period, extending from age 6 or 7 to puberty, then sets in.

Freud felt that the "castration complex," anxiety aroused by a perceived fear of loss of the male genital organs, was the basic cause of repression of the Oedipal sexual feelings toward the mother, and thus led to the onset of the latency period. When libidinous drives reawaken at adolescence, however, the adolescent is likely to experience conflict and maladjustments if he has unresolved problems from any of the earlier stages.

Modifications and reformulations of the Freudian view

The personality development picture in Freudian theory is very much a social-psychological one, with the child-parent relationships central, although Freud dealt with many phenomena in this development process as if they were instinctive, biologically inevitable phenomena. Current views in social psychology would be likely to interpret the same phenomena in terms of the dynamics of interpersonal behavior within the family.

For example, Freud's view of the Oedipus complex was that there is an inevitable, unconscious sexual desire toward the parent of the opposite sex and a resentment of the parent of the same sex, the latter being accompanied by both fear and love. Such ambivalence of the son toward the father and the libidinous desire of the son toward the mother were repressed and led to later unconscious conflict. The phenomenon of father-son rivalry and of mother-son attraction is real enough, and was probably a prominent contributor to the conflicts of Freud's Victorian-era patients. But the existence of the Oedipus complex and its form are a function of the culture within which the child is being socialized. Specifically, it is a function of the pattern of behaviors of parents toward each other and the child, and of their expectations for the child's behavior.

Let us consider the Hopi Indians as an illustration (Aberle, 1951). The Hopi kinship system is such that the child's biological father is a loving playmate to his sons while the mother's elder brother administers all punishment and discipline. In our current culture, on the other hand, the father is both loving playmate and disciplinarian, often nearly at one and the same time. The kind of role system of the Hopi family leads to far less love/fear ambivalence by the child toward his father than does our American family-role system.

Many of Freud's concepts can be reformulated in this way, with em-

phasis on the social interaction within the family and less stress upon the biological determinism of the process. The successive erogenous stages are, in fact, the successive foci of child-parent interaction: feeding, toilet training, and the child's exploratory behavior. Personality as it develops is a function of the parents' way of interacting with the child on these focal-problem areas. For example, whether or not autoeroticism is suppressed depends on the particular culture. In some societies, it is not suppressed and is even encouraged; the fondling of the baby's genitalia is a normal part of adult play relationships with him, just as in our society mothers play "this little piggie" with the child's toes. Thus, the castration complex may not be inevitable, but may be an anxiety that arises when and if the autoerotic activities of the early childhood period are sharply repressed. Furthermore, there is no latency period in some societies and no equivalent of the Oedipus complex in others.

A neo-Freudian psychoanalyst, E. H. Erikson (1950), has described the development of the normal personality in terms of a series of eight focal problems or dilemmas. These roughly parallel the Freudian stages but continue on into adulthood. Erikson's emphasis, however, is more clearly on the social interaction process and its outcome. His eight basic problems are: (1) basic trust versus basic mistrust (oral); (2) autonomy versus shame and doubt (anal); (3) initiative versus guilt (phallic); (4) industry versus inferiority (latency); (5) identity versus self-diffusion (puberty); (6) intimacy versus self-absorption (early adulthood); (7) generativity versus stagnation (later adulthood); (8) integrity versus despair (old age).

Each of these problems poses a crisis for the developing personality. The ego may succumb to any one of these crises, this leading to particular abnormalities related to that problem. If the ego does not succumb to the crisis but becomes fixated upon it in continuing attempts to solve it, it will be more easily overwhelmed by the next crisis. The healthy individual must satisfactorily solve each of these problems through parent-child, and later child-peer, interaction.

Many other theorists have developed pictures of the dynamics of personality development. Most of the more recent theories (for example, Horney, 1939; Mullahy, 1952; Fromm, 1941) stress the interactive nature of the process. The central theme is that personality develops by a process of social learning (socialization) in which the parents impose the standards of the society upon the child (selectively), and he in turn adjusts to these constraints as to when and how he may satisfy his basic biological drives (hunger, thirst, sex, aggression, and others). The pattern of this adjustment process *is* the development of personality. It is continuous, though the early years are the most crucial. It is dynamic. It is unique

to each individual. It is interactive, depending on the unique pattern of the relationships that develop between a particular child and his particular parents, for parents are themselves unique personalities who interpret the cultural patterns in their own idiosyncratic way as they participate in the process of socialization.

SUPPLEMENTARY READING

Attitudes and Motives

Festinger, L. *A theory of cognitive dissonance.* New York: Harper & Row, Publishers, 1957.

Fishbein, M., & Raven, B. H. An operational distinction between belief and attitude. Los Angeles: University of California Press, 1959. [Tech. Rep. No. 2, Contract Nonr 233(54).]

Hovland, C. I., Janis, I. L., & Kelley, H. H. *Communication and persuasion.* New Haven, Conn.: Yale University Press, 1953.

Murphy, G. Social motivation. In G. Lindzey (Ed.), *Handbook of social psychology.* Reading, Mass.: Addison-Wesley Publishing Company, Inc., 1954. Chap. 16.

Maccoby, E. E., Newcomb, T. M., & Hartley, E. L. *Readings in social psychology.* New York: Holt, Rinehart and Winston, Inc., 1958. Especially readings by:

> Katz, D., & Braly, K. W. Verbal stereotypes and racial prejudice, pp. 40–46.
>
> Lewin, K. Group decision and social change, pp. 197–211.
>
> Lumsdaine, A. A., & Janis, I. L. Resistance to "counterpropaganda" produced by one-sided and two-sided "propaganda" presentations, pp. 131–136.
>
> Pelz, E. B. Some factors in "Group Decision," pp. 212–218.

Perception, Language, and Interpersonal Perception

Bruner, J. S., & Tagiuri, R. The perception of people. In G. Lindzey (Ed.), *Handbook of social psychology.* Reading, Mass.: Addison-Wesley Publishing Company, Inc., 1954. Chap. 17.

Maccoby, E. E., Newcomb, T. M., & Hartley, E. L. *Readings in social psychology.* New York: Holt, Rinehart and Winston, Inc., 1958. Especially readings by:

> Bruner, J. S. Social psychology and perception, pp. 85–93.
>
> Whorf, B. L. Science and linguistics, pp. 1–8.

Newcomb, T. M. An approach to the study of communicative acts. *Psychol. Rev.*, 1953, *4*, 183–214.

Osgood, C. E., Suci, G. J., & Tannenbaum, P. H. *The measurement of meaning.* Urbana, Ill.: University of Illinois Press, 1957.

Tagiuri, R., & Petrullo, L. *Person perception and interpersonal behavior.* Stanford, Calif.: Stanford University Press, 1958.

Socialization and Personality Development

Child, I. L. Socialization. In G. Lindzey (Ed.), *Handbook of social psychology.* Reading, Mass.: Addison-Wesley Publishing Company, Inc., 1954. Chap. 18.

Erikson, E. H. *Childhood and society.* New York: W. W. Norton & Company, Inc., 1950.

Hall, C. S., & Lindzey, G. *Theories of personality.* New York: John Wiley & Sons, Inc., 1957.

McClelland, D. C. *Personality.* New York: Holt, Rinehart and Winston, Inc., 1951.

Maccoby, E. E., Newcomb, T. M., & Hartley, E. L. *Readings in social psychology.* New York: Holt, Rinehart and Winston, Inc., 1958. Especially readings by:

> Bronfenbrenner, U. Socialization and social class through time and space, pp. 400–424.
>
> Sears, R. R., Maccoby, E. E., & Levin, H. The socialization of aggression, pp. 350–359.
>
> Whiting, J. W. M., Kluckhohn, R., & Anthony, A. The function of male initiation ceremonies at puberty, pp. 359–370.

PART THREE /

The Group

Why study groups?

We have learned that individuals are what they are largely because they have undergone a social learning process, which we called socialization. This social learning process occurs in an interactive context. Initially, it takes place in the family; later it occurs in other groups such as school and play groups. Thus, the society as a whole does not directly participate in the socialization process for any given individual. Rather, the "significant others" in that child's environment, as agents of the society, are instrumental in his socialization.

Since the major shaping of the individual takes place within an interactive context, an understanding of the process requires that we explore

61

the nature of face-to-face interactive groups. Hence, we will turn our attention to the small group as an entity.

There is another equally important reason for studying groups. Groups and other collectivities exhibit properties from which we can reasonably conclude that they are relatively autonomous "systems" worthy of study in their own right. For example, some groups have a continuity of existence that extends beyond the membership period, or even the life span, of individual members. They have traditions, customs, and a division of labor that cannot literally be attributed to any one or several individual members. Above all, there is usually a recognition by members of the existence of "the group" as a meaningful entity, accompanied by an in-group or "we-feeling" among members. Thus, we study groups because these and other phenomena, which can only be studied at the group level, are important social psychological phenomena in themselves.

CHAPTER 7

/ An approach to
the study of groups

Early experimental studies of the effects of groups concerned themselves with the question of whether individuals perform better when working alone or when working in the presence of others. In these early studies, the "group" variable being studied was the mere presence and activity of other people, not any direct interaction among those people. Results of studies of such "coacting" groups showed that working in the presence of others tended to increase speed and decrease quality (accuracy) of individual performance, even when the experimental conditions were arranged so as to eliminate or reduce the effects of rivalry. These early results were interpreted as arising from a literal summation effect of increased sensory stimulation, the sights and sounds of other persons working on the same task. They are often referred to as the phenomenon of "social facilitation" (for example, F. Allport, 1920).

Somewhat later, research in this area began to focus on task performance in interacting (rather than coacting) groups. In studies of problem solving by groups, Marjorie Shaw (1932) found that groups, as compared with individuals working alone, solved more problems correctly; had fewer errors, especially in early stages of work on the problem; and worked with as much speed as the average individual, although not always with as much speed as the fastest individual. These results suggest that groups may be superior in problem solving partly because a group provides checks and balances against the occurrence of errors. However, later related studies (Taylor & Faust, 1952; Taylor *et al.*, 1957) show also that the relative effectiveness of individuals versus groups in any task activity is highly dependent on the nature of the task.

In the last few decades, research on small groups has blossomed into a large and relatively autonomous area of study. Along with this growth have come several major shifts in emphasis. First, while research on the effects of a group on its individual members has continued, there has been far greater concern with the study of groups as such. That is, as the small group has become a subject of study in its own right, emphasis has shifted from concern with the performance and adjustment of group members to a concern with the group's structure, the process of interaction in which it engages, and the performance of the group as a group. Another major shift has been toward the development of more rigorous and more precise methods for measuring group characteristics and behavior and for conducting experiments on groups. Considerable advance has been made also in the rigor of formulation of theory and in a closer coordination between theoretical development and experimental tests of theory.

Even though major research effort has been devoted to the study of small group behavior and substantial advances in theory and method have been made, the small group field is still in a relatively embryonic state. A clear statement of basic principles or a clear formulation of the basic properties of groups does not yet exist. Above all, an adequate theoretical formulation for the area has still to be developed. The remainder of Part Three will attempt to lay out some of the more important concepts and findings in the small group area and relate them to one another and to the material of Part Two. So that our presentation may be fairly clear and concise, we must again impose a structure, or frame of reference, on the material, though this will tend to give an oversimplified picture of a complex area of study.

Generally, the study of groups has been approached from three different perspectives. The first views the group as a medium within which to study the (social) behavior of the individual. This is primarily a psychological approach: the study of the behavior of individuals in a group environment. The second approach is the attempt to identify key properties of groups as groups and investigate the effects of differences in these group properties. This is primarily a sociological perspective. The third approach, which is more nearly a social psychological one, attempts to study the interplay between the group as a functional entity and the individuals who are its members. We will mainly be concerned with the latter approach, after a brief discussion of some global properties of groups.

Group properties

We have already noted the variety and complexity of behavior of individual human beings. In our everyday lives we can observe also tremendous variation among groups. We encounter many groups: families, work groups, friendship groups, formal and informal associations of many kinds. No two groups that we experience are exactly alike, just as no two individuals are exactly alike.

Yet, as with individuals, we may often be impressed by marked similarities, as well as by differences, among groups. Just as we can detect common properties along which individuals vary, so it is likely that we can find common properties of groups which can be used to describe how groups differ from one another.

It is relatively easy to list a fairly large number of properties which are descriptive of groups (for example, Hemphill, 1949). Groups may differ in:

1. Size, or the number of members
2. The degree to which they are organized and operate in a formal manner
3. The degree to which they are stratified, that is, the extent to which group members are related to one another in a hierarchy
4. The degree to which they exercise or attempt to exercise control over the behavior of their members
5. The degree of participation which is permitted, expected, or demanded of members
6. The ease of access to membership in the group and the ease with which a member can leave or be expelled from the group
7. The degree of stability of the group over time and the continuity of its membership over time
8. The degree to which group members relate to one another intimately, on a personal basis and with respect to a wide range of activities and interests, rather than in a formal manner and only with respect to a narrowly defined set of activities
9. The degree to which the group is subdivided into smaller groups or cliques, and the extent to which such cliques are in conflict with one another

Some of these differences among groups have important consequences for group action and its results. For example, increases in group size tend

to be accompanied by increased centralization of authority, increased for-
mality of group operation, increased differences among members in participation and satisfaction, and the need for increased leadership skill for
effective group performance. Such differences tend to be related to size
in a "diminishing returns" type of function; that is, a given absolute difference in size (say, the addition of one more member) makes more
difference for smaller groups, less difference for larger groups. Thus, there
are substantial differences between two-person and three-person groups;
differences between three- and four-person groups are less sharp; differences between four- and five-man groups are still less. Hare (1952) has
shown substantial differences between five- and twelve-man groups. There
probably are no major differences between twelve- and fourteen-man
groups, or even between seventeen- and twenty-three–man groups. One
reason for this diminishing-returns type of function for increasing size of
group is that as groups get larger they tend to subdivide into smaller
subgroups or cliques. Sometimes this is done formally, as a "division of
labor" or an "organization." Sometimes it occurs informally.

Thus, a very large number of properties have or can be used to characterize groups and examine differences among them. Such extensive lists,
like lists of personality traits, are of relatively little use, however, unless
the items are somehow related to one another by means of integrating
theoretical constructs. We do not yet have a comprehensive and useful
set of group properties; nor do we have a viable typology of groups. Ac-
cordingly, in order to progress with our examination of the nature of
groups and their consequences, it is necessary to state and define certain
concepts that can be used as analytic tools in our inquiry.

Groups as role systems

Normally, we tend to think of groups as sets of individual
members; that is, we think of the *parts* of a group as being the individual
persons who are its members. This way of conceptualizing groups is probably not too useful for purposes of systematic study. For one thing, social
scientists who have worked from this viewpoint have not had much success in identifying major group properties or in tracing the consequences
of differences in those properties. Furthermore, it is apparent that an
individual is not a "part" of any given group in the same sense that an
atom "belongs" to a particular molecule or that a chair leg belongs to a
particular chair. That is, no one person belongs to a given group totally
and to no other group. Rather, individuals belong to (are a part of) many
groups simultaneously. The individual *participates in,* rather than belongs

to, each of a series of groups. Thus, it may not be very useful to conceptualize the individual member as the basic unit or part of which a group is composed.

As an alternative view, we can think of a group as a "system" of interrelated parts, where the parts are not individual members as such but are *roles*. To explain this way of conceptualizing groups, we must introduce and define several related concepts: positions, roles, role relationships, role expectations, and role behaviors. Our definitions here follow largely those of Newcomb (1950). Other researchers (such as Linton, 1945) define some of these terms differently.

Every person belongs to a variety of groups, formal and informal: family, work groups, clubs, informal friendship groups, and others. Persons who take part in such groups can be viewed as having different *positions*—or niches or jobs—in them. In some groups, the positions are clear-cut and named. For example, in a family we readily distinguished between the positions of father, mother, son, daughter. Often, we make further distinctions of position; for example, the oldest son and other sons. In a work situation, we distinguish between such positions as department head, section chief, treasurer, supervisor, worker. In other groups, such positions are less clear-cut but nevertheless can be distinguished if we observe the groups closely. For example, in an informal friendship group there is often one person who sets goals for the group and to whom others generally turn for decisions. He could be considered as occupying the position of leader in that group even though he might not be formally designated as group leader.

Many positions in groups are recognized on a broader, community basis rather than just within one small face-to-face group. These "institutionalized" positions include political positions (mayor or congressman), occupational positions (clergyman, physician, student, or attorney), and other socially defined positions (teenager, citizen, or criminal).

Any position in a group or a community implies the existence of certain related positions and, further, that there is a certain relationship between the person in one position and persons occupying other related positions. For example, the position of mother implies the position of child. It also implies a certain kind of relationship between the person who is mother and the person who is child. We will call the relationship of the mother to the child the *role* of mother. We will call the *dual and reciprocal* relationship of mother to child and child to mother as the mother-child *role relationship*.

A person in the position of mother (the female member of the adult pair who are the head of a family) has a whole *set* of roles that stem from that position. She is mother to her child, wife to her husband, daughter-in-law to her husband's mother, family representative to the P.T.A. and to salesmen. Each of these are distinctive sets of reciprocal relationships. Even though all these role relationships arise because of her position in the family, each is a different role for her, since each requires different kinds of behaviors toward the person at the other end of the relationship.

When we consider the allocation of individuals to positions, we can identify two main ways that persons come to occupy certain positions (with accompanying roles) and not others. *Ascribed* positions and roles are those the individual comes to occupy (or to be excluded from) because of some inherent or immutable characteristic such as age, sex, race, caste or class. *Achieved* positions and roles are those the individual acquires on the basis of his performance and his choice. Most occupational roles (attorney, carpenter, department head, clergyman) in our society are achieved rather than ascribed, although this is not necessarily the case for occupational roles in other cultures.

It is important to distinguish between the behaviors expected of a person in a particular role and the behavior a particular person actually exhibits while acting in that role. To say that there is a role of mother implies that we expect a person in that role to act in a certain way vis-à-vis her child. These expectations include certain prescriptions (things the person must do), and certain prohibitions (things the person must not do), as well as a range of less strictly defined expectations (the things the person ought to do in that role). For example, to acceptably perform the role of mother, a woman "must" love her child; she "must not" administer excessively violent punishments to him; she "ought to" train him in certain kinds of behavior. We will call the prescriptions and prohibitions associated with a given role the *role expectations* for that role.

We can distinguish between the role expectations and the actual behaviors of a given person in a given role. The *role behavior* of any person in a given role may or may not match or fulfill the expectations which he and others in related roles hold for incumbents of that role. In fact, we tend to view our own role behavior and the role behavior of others in relation to our expectations for that behavior, and to *evaluate* the person(s) involved on the basis of that comparison. We will have more to say (see Chapter 11) about the problems that can arise as persons attempt to meet their own role expectations and role expectations of others for their behavior.

We have been talking about positions, roles, and role relationships from the point of view of the individual. If we consider these same concepts from the point of view of a group, we are talking about *group structure*. Group structure, as used here, refers to the pattern of role relationships within a group. For example, the group structure of a family with one child includes the *set* of reciprocal role relationships: mother–child, father–child, and husband–wife. The group structure of a work group may include superordinate—subordinate relationships and coworker or peer relationships at each of several levels or echelons. It may also include more complex relationships, such as staff–line, administrator–technical specialist, adviser–policy makers. Thus, group structure refers to *the set of related positions in a group and the total patterns of role relationships among the occupants of those positions.* In this sense, we can view groups as systems of interrelated positions and roles.

Of course, in viewing groups as role systems, we must not lose sight of the fact that individual human beings fulfill the roles in a human group. Thus, we must not view the group's network of positions and related roles as if it were a set of mechanically connected "components," and as if performance of the group were totally predictable from knowledge of the pattern of connections and the "specifications" for each component. Role behavior is affected greatly by role expectations, but it is also greatly affected by the personality of the occupant of the role. We will turn now to a brief statement of the basic frame of reference within which we will organize our discussion of groups and their effects.

A frame of reference for analysis of groups

In order to deal in a clear and orderly fashion with the myriad factors, or variables, involved in the study of groups, it is useful to aggregate them into sets that have a lot in common. Any classification of variables within a complex problem area amounts to an oversimplification of reality, and the present one is no exception. Such a classification of variables can be useful, however, if it preserves the basic concepts and simplifies discussion of them. It is even more useful if the classes of variables are related to one another in some logical manner. The classification of variables that we shall use and some of the logical relations among them are shown in Figure 2 and discussed below. (The same classification of variables will be presented in more detail in Figure 4, page 114.)

A group refers to a set of human beings who are its members. These members, distributively, have various properties: abilities, attitudes, background characteristics (such as sex and age), and personality characteristics. We can think of these individual properties collectively as the group's *composition*. Group composition can be dealt with at three levels of complexity. First, we can ask about the *level* or total amount of any property possessed by all members combined; for example, their average

age or average intelligence. Second, we can consider the *homogeneity* or similarity among members with respect to any given property; for example, how alike their political attitudes are, whether all members are male or it is a mixed sex group. Third, if there is not total homogeneity, we can ask about the *compatibility* among members for any given property; for example, whether their personality characteristics "clash" or fit together well.

Groups are also made up of *relationships among members.* These include relationships among the members as people, namely, friendship relationships, and relationships among members as occupants of positions: their role relationships, in terms of activity, power, and communication. The pattern of differentiation and the network of connections among members and among roles can be thought of as the *group structure.*

The group exists within an environment and has a set of goals or reasons

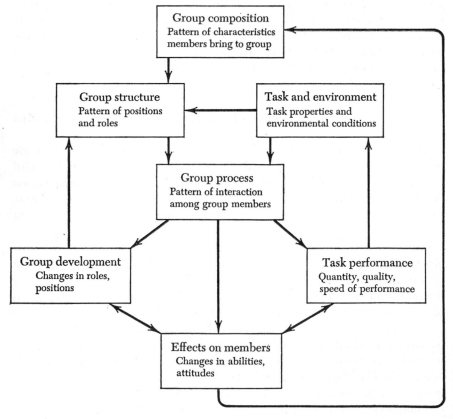

FIGURE 2   Frame of Reference for Analysis of Groups.

for existence, which we will call the group's *task*. Tasks vary in their properties; hence, they vary in the performance requirements they impose on the group. Variations in properties of the physical and social environment also affect the group's operation.

We will use the term *group process* to refer to the activities of members and the interactions among them as the group performs its task within its environmental setting. The group process is shaped by the interplay of aspects of its composition and structure, and the demands of the task and environment.

Group process yields three kinds of effects. First, it leads to alterations in the group's relation to its goals and to its environment. We will refer to these results as *task performance*. Secondly, group process leads to alterations in the patterns of relationship among members and among roles, and to the development of shared beliefs, attitudes, goals, and ways of perceiving. We will refer to these effects as *group development*. Just as task performance implies an alteration in the group's relation to its environment, group development implies alterations in the group itself. Finally, group process leads to alterations in properties of members—in abilities, attitudes, even personality. We will refer to these results as *effects on members*.

These three kinds of effects of group process are potential in any group situation. They represent alteration in group members, the group itself, and the group's relation to its environment. Thus, the effects of group process at one time alter the antecedent conditions that will shape the group process at subsequent times. This way of looking at groups deals with group phenomena as a recurrent cycle of "input, process and output," in which the output, or results, at one point in time alters the input conditions for the next period of time, and these in turn alter subsequent group process and its results. Figure 2 outlines the stages in only one cycle of a continuous process.

In Chapter 8 we will discuss various aspects of group structure and composition. Chapter 9 will be devoted to leadership, which is a special aspect of group composition and structure but one that has received so much attention in the past that it merits separate treatment. Chapter 10 deals with group process, the pattern of interaction among members. Chapter 11 discusses the three kinds of group effects: task performance, group development, and the effects on individual members.

CHAPTER 8

/ *Group composition and structure*

In this chapter we will consider differences in group composition and structure and the effects of these differences on the group and its members.

Group composition refers to the properties represented by the aggregate of persons who are the members of a given group at a given time. We can consider group composition with respect to any of the many variables in terms of which we can characterize individuals: abilities, attitudes, personality characteristics, or personal attributes such as age, sex, educational background, and others.

Group structure refers to the relatively stable patterns of relationships that exist among members of groups. As the term is used here, all groups can be described in terms of many aspects of their structure, even groups of relatively short duration. Group structure, like "personality," is not something that different groups have or do not have, or that different groups have more or less of. Rather, groups differ in the kind or form of structure they have, just as individuals may differ in the kind or form of personality structure by which they can be characterized.

If we define groups as sets of interlocked roles, we cannot merely list a set of roles that form the "parts" for all groups. Rather, each group or type of group is likely to have a different set of particular roles. We can specify much of the role structure of a family in terms of the position and roles of father-husband, mother-wife, son-brother, and daughter-sister. These particular role relationships would be meaningless for describing the role structure of a work group or of an athletic team. It is possible, however, to describe at least three major dimensions in terms of which *any* set of roles may be *differentiated from* one another and *related to* one another. For each dimension, if we focus on the individual role as it is related to other roles, we are dealing with basic properties of roles; while if we focus on the total pattern of relationships among roles, we are dealing with different forms of group structure. The three dimensions of role relationships are:

1. Role differences in terms of task activities or responsibilities: the *work structure*
2. Role differences in terms of authority or influence: the *power structure*
3. Role differences in terms of communication channels: the *communication structure*

One further dimension of group structure has to do with relations among members, rather than among roles:

4. The pattern of affect relations among members: the *friendship structure*

Before we consider these patterns of group structure, we will discuss group composition, that is, the sets of abilities, attitudes, and other properties members bring with them to the group.

Composition of the group

What a group is and what it does depends in part on characteristics of its members, independent of the role structure of the group. For example, a group of men with high ability can certainly do a task better than a group with lower ability. It does not always follow, however, that the group with higher ability will do the task better. If the task does not demand much skill, the additional ability of the better group will be superfluous and might even be detrimental if the task were so easy and unchallenging that the group had little motivation to perform it. Thus, a group does not necessarily need the *highest possible* levels of ability in all members. What it needs is a *distribution* of levels and types of abilities which best fits the requirements of its task.

Furthermore, the task, power, or communication structure of a group may operate to prevent the effective utilization of abilities of members. Torrance (1954) found that the effectiveness of group actions in a new and ambiguous situation (a physical-survival situation) was influenced adversely for groups whose prior power structure (the formal rank structure of air crews) remained unaltered. The formal structure of the crew, designed to perform a different task, tended to prevent the utilization of skills and resources of members who were low in that formal structure but had high levels of skills relevant to the new situation. Fiedler and Meuwese (1963) found evidence that the utilization of member abilities depends on the type of formal leader and his style of leadership. Several studies of groups with restricted communication structures, which will be discussed later in this chapter, indicate that the degree to which the group gets the benefit of the skills of a particular member depends on the position of that member (how central he is) in the communication structure. Thus, while it is probably true that when all other things are equal groups of more able men perform tasks better than groups of less able men, there are many factors besides the task skills of members which affect group performance.

A group's effectiveness depends also on the *personalities* of its members. But just what kinds of personalities make for good groups? "Folklore" on this question supports either one of two opposite premises: (1) that persons with *similar* personalities make good groups, as in "Birds of a feather flock together"; or (2) that persons with *different* personalities make good groups, as in "Opposites attract." Recently, Schutz (1958) tested the hypothesis that persons with *different but complementary* patterns on certain personality characteristics are most compatible, hence make the most effective groups. He combined pairs of people in terms of the strength of their needs to give and to receive inclusion (belongingness), control, and affection. The compatible pairs were those in which member A had a high need to give inclusion, control, and/or affection to others, while member B had a high need to receive inclusion, control, and/or affection. He compared such compatible groups with pairs in which the two members had similar patterns of these needs (for example, both members had high needs to give affection or inclusion or control), and with other pairs whose members had different but noncomplementary patterns of needs (e.g., member A had a high need to give control while member B had a high need to receive affection). He found the compatible pairs to be more effective on relatively complex group problem-solving tasks, although the different types of groups were about equal on easy tasks.

Other research on homogeneity of personality does not provide a very clear picture. Cohen (1956) studied the performance of two-person groups whose members were either similar or dissimilar in their preferred defense mechanism (projection, aggression, repression, and so on). He found that groups in which both members tended to use projection as a preferred defense mechanism performed less effectively, but he did not find any consistent differences for groups that were either similar or dissimilar in the use of other defense mechanisms. Haythorn *et al.* (1956) and Altman and McGinnies (1960) found that there was less intragroup hostility in groups whose members were homogeneous in attitudes toward authority. On the other hand, Hoffman (1959) has shown that task performance was better for groups whose members were heterogeneous in over-all personality patterns.

The conflicting evidence makes it probable that neither homogeneity nor heterogeneity of members per se is desirable. Rather, it is likely that homogeneity on some characteristics and heterogeneity on others make for effective groups. Homogeneity on certain personality characteristics such as dominance or the use of projection will almost certainly be disruptive in a group; homogeneity on other characteristics, such as sociability, may lead to greater member satisfactions and smoother cooperation on the task. Homogeneity or heterogeneity on other personality variables may make no difference at all.

Regarding member abilities, performance is likely to be better if a group has a heterogeneity of skills, or at least a distribution of skills that is of sufficient range to deal with all required tasks, than if it has a narrower range of skills common to all members. On the other hand, groups whose members have similar backgrounds and hence similar attitudes and values are likely to have better communication and better affect relations. For example, Fiedler, Meuwese, and Oonk (1961) found less friction and better performance in groups homogeneous in religious background. Here again, however, there are probably many specific background factors and attitudes for which the degree of member homogeneity or heterogeneity does not matter.

Another crucial aspect of group composition has to do with the level and diversity of the *motivations* of group members. Groups differ from one another in terms of how strongly motivated their members are, collectively, with respect to attaining the group's goals. Furthermore, it is unlikely that all members of any given group will be equally strongly motivated toward achievement of the group's goals. Both levels of over-all member motivation and differences in intensity of motivation among group members will affect how well the group can accomplish its objectives. As with levels of ability, adequate levels of motivation of group members are a necessary but not a sufficient condition for group success. A poorly motivated group will almost certainly not be highly successful on relatively difficult tasks. A highly motivated group, however, may or may not be successful, depending on the level and distribution of member abilities, the pattern of member personality characteristics, and whether the group's task, power, communication, and friendship structures aid or hinder task performance.

Perhaps a more crucial aspect of group-member motivation has to do with whether or not group members are motivated toward group goals rather than individual goals. In any group situation, the individual is to some extent engaged in the business of satisfying his own motivations. Sometimes the individual motivations are such that all members want the same *collective* outcomes, that is, they *share* the same goals for the group. For example, business partners committed to a 50–50 split of costs and profits presumably share the goal of group profit. What is in the best (economic) interests of the group is also in their own individual best interests. In other situations, the individual motivations of group members may not converge on the same goals and may in fact be incompatible.

In large measure, the motivations of individual group members depend on the nature of the rewards members hope to attain through group membership and group activity, the manner in which rewards are related to task performance, and the way in which rewards for group success are distributed among group members. We can distinguish at least three patterns in which individual and group performance and individual and group rewards can be related.

First, group members can receive rewards on the basis of their individual performances, without regard to the task performance of other members. In such a situation, group members are independent, rather than interdependent, at least with regard to their motivation–task performance–reward patterns.

Second, group members can be striving for rewards under conditions where the more one member gains the less others can gain. Here, the members are interdependent but are in competition for rewards. This condition has been termed *contriant interdependence* (Thomas, 1957).

Third, group members can be striving for rewards under conditions where the more one member gains the more all others gain as well. Here, members are interdependent but can gain rewards best if they cooperate with one another. This condition has been called *facilitative interdependence* (Thomas, 1957). Deutsch (1949), Mintz (1951), Thomas (1957), and others have shown that group task performance, as well as interpersonal relations among group members, are better under conditions of facilitative interdependence, where the motivational conditions tend to foster cooperative behavior, than under conditions of contriant interdependence, where the motivational conditions tend to foster competition among group members.

A fourth pattern can also occur. Group members can be striving for rewards that stem from interpersonal relationships as such and that are not contingent on the group's task success. Under these conditions, task performance of group members is unrelated to their rewards and the rewards of others, but group members are highly interdependent for the rewards that stem from pleasant interpersonal relations.

Group structure: Patterns of role relationships

1. WORK STRUCTURE AND THE TASK

The most obvious way to describe a set of roles is in terms of the part each role plays in the group's activity. When we consider the group's division of labor, or division of task responsibilities, we may focus on the nature of the separate roles (such as task specialization) or on the pattern by which the set of task roles are integrated (for example, the bases for subgroupings of roles; the mechanisms for coordination between roles or sets of roles). This differentiation and integration of roles with respect to task activities is one major basis for describing the structure of a group.

The subject of division of labor and its consequences has been of concern in our society for many years. Much has been said about the advantages and disadvantages of task specialization. The main argument in favor of specialization has usually been based on the assumption that it makes for efficiency of·task performance. If each man performs a limited set of activities for which he is highly trained, a set of specialists working together can accomplish a total job which involves so many diverse skills that no one man could have them all. This is one basic premise on which our modern, highly specialized, technologically sophisticated civilization has been built.

The main argument against task specialization has been in terms of its effects on individuals as human beings. The basic premise of this argument is that the satisfaction obtained from task accomplishment is an important factor in human adjustment and that such satisfaction is greatly reduced when the individual performs only a single, specific task operation and thus does not experience a feeling of accomplishment. This side effect of our industrial revolution has been considered a major cause of problems of individual adjustment in our modern world.

In spite of all the concern and discussion of the effects of task specialization, we still do not have much *scientific* knowledge (as opposed to opinion) about those effects. There is little evidence that task specialization as such affects individual morale or adjustment, although there is convincing evidence that being relatively isolated in the communication pattern of a work group does have such negative effects. We also have evidence that participation in decisions affecting one's job yields more favorable attitudes and better performance (see Coch & French, 1948; Mulder, 1959). But communication isolation and lack of opportunity to make job decisions are not necessary parts of task specialization.

There is little evidence about the task performance effects of specialization. It is doubtless true that large and complex tasks can be accomplished better if they are divided among several people and that a task will not be done at all if no one who is available has the ability to do it. We do not know, however, how best to divide up any particular task into specialized jobs. Such a division must reckon with at least three facets of the problem. First, the division of jobs must relate closely to the distribution of skills among the people who do the jobs. For example, if all elementary school teachers were trained as specialists in only one subject, we would have to use a team-teaching system rather than a homeroom-teacher system. Secondly, the division of jobs must be made so that the jobs tie in well together; we must be sure that completion of task A is all that is required before task B can be carried out. Third, we must divide tasks so that they can be efficiently coordinated in time and space. The efficiency of task specialization is lost, for example, if an automobile manufacturer ends up with 30,000 motors and only 10,000 bodies.

A great deal of "applied" research has been done on task differentiation and coordination in industrial and military settings. Early efforts on these problems were called time and motion studies and grew out of F. W. Taylor's (1911) crusade for scientific management. Later efforts have been carried out under the headings of operations research and recently systems research. Unfortunately, however, most of this research is particularistic, that is, geared to determine the best division and coordination of activity for a *particular* complex task (such as the launching of a particular missile). Hence, it does not add much to our *general* knowledge of the effects of different work-structure patterns.

Research on the more general problem of work structure is fairly scarce. Lanzetta and Roby (1956) have compared two general types of work structure: a *horizontal* division of labor, in which each man handles the several different parts of a group task but does so for only one portion of the group's area of responsibility; and a *vertical* division of labor, in which each man handles only one part of the group's task but does so for the group's entire area of responsibility. They found the former to be slightly more efficient, especially for reasonably light work loads, but this difference was *reversed* for heavier work loads. While differences were not strong, they suggest that the best division of labor even for a particular task depends partly on work load.

The Lanzetta and Roby study is based on the condition that every man has the necessary skills to perform all tasks involved. This is often not the case, especially for groups performing highly specialized tasks requiring extensive training.

The nature of the group's task interacts with the group's work structure. The kind of task the group is performing affects the kinds of activity and coordination required, and this in turn affects the choice of the most appropriate division of labor. A wide variety of tasks have been studied in small group research, but relatively little systematic investigation has been done of the properties of the tasks themselves.

Carter *et al.* (1950) studied group performance on a number of tasks and concluded that from the point of view of effective leadership there are at least two distinct kinds of group tasks: intellectual tasks and manual, or "do with the hands," tasks. Many further distinctions can be made within the global category of intellectual tasks. For example, many researchers have distinguished between problem solving and creative tasks (for example, Fiedler, 1962). Problem-solving tasks require the group to *integrate* various pieces of information into "the" solution, or the best solution. Creative tasks require the group to *generate* a number of original ideas about a topic. Some tasks, of course, require both the generation of new ideas and their synthesis into a coherent solution. We can distinguish also another type of intellectual task, negotiation tasks, which require members to *integrate divergent attitudes or values* rather than generate or integrate information.

It would appear that such task differences, which require different patterns of task activity and interaction among members, may also require different patterns of role differentiation and coordination. Recently, Shaw (1963) proposed a set of ten dimensions for describing and differentiating a wide range of group tasks. These include such properties as single versus multiple paths to goal; clarity of the relationship between path and goal; specificity versus generality of the solution. These dimensions offer a substantial refinement of the gross categories of intellectual versus manual tasks and problem-solving versus creative tasks. Such a schema, when fully elaborated, may make it possible to compare results obtained on various group tasks and to explore relationships between type of task and the group's division of labor.

Analytically, we can specify the *connection* between task roles of any two people as one of several types: (1) *A* and *B* can do the same task, while working independently (for example, Lanzetta and Roby's horizontal structure, or tellers at adjacent windows in a bank); (2) A and B can work on separate, sequential steps of the same task, so that A's output provides B's input (Lanzetta and Roby's vertical structure, or workers at adjacent stations on an assembly line); (3) A and B can work on complementary aspects of the same task simultaneously (a blocker and a ball carrier on a football team, or the members of a land-survey team); (4) B may direct or supervise the activities of A.

These types of task connections have different implications for the degree to which A and B are dependent on each other for their activities. In type 1, A and B are unrelated; their task performances are independent. In type 2, B is dependent on A, because an error in performance by A disrupts B's task performance. In type 3, A and B are interdependent; the performance of each affects the requirements placed on the other. In type 4, A is dependent on B for direction of his work and in terms of its evaluation, but B is dependent on A in another sense, because A must do part of the job for which B is responsible. Such task relations between group members also affect the influence relations and the communication relations that are likely to develop between them.

2. POWER STRUCTURE

The set of roles within a group may be described in terms of the relative authority or *power* of each role. In a formal group, each role can be designated as to its position in an authority or power hierarchy, and as to its superordinate or subordinate relation to other roles. In informal groups, differentiations in power are likely to be equally prominent though less explicitly defined.

There are many forms or bases of power. French and Raven (1959) define power as the *potential* influence of person O on person P in a particular area. They distinguish five bases of power: (1) reward power; (2) coercive power; (3) legitimate power, such as the "right" of a formally chosen leader to direct the actions of members; (4) referent power, or power based on P's liking for or identification with O; and (5) power based on expert knowledge. Even in informal and transient groups, members tend to differ in their relative power (potential influence). Degree of power tends to correlate with the holding of a position of formal leadership, but is by no means entirely a matter of such formal authority. The degree of power O has over P is also related to his friendship or affect relations with P. A group (or one of its members) can have power to influence a particular member P to the extent that P is attracted to that group, that is, to the extent that the group can provide or withhold rewards which are valuable to P.

Sometimes the power of a role derives from the status of the person who happens to occupy that role in the group. By "status" we mean the prestige the individual possesses as a person, independent of his position in a particular group. Such status can arise from the person's general social status (wealth or position of prestige) or from specific features of his background such as age, sex, race, education. (The latter are the institutionalized positions he occupies in the general society.) Strodtbeck and his associates (1957) have shown that both males and persons of higher socioeconomic status have more influence in jury deliberations than females or persons of lower socioeconomic status (see page 101).

Hurwitz and his associates (1960) found that persons representing higher-status professions (such as medicine) in an interdisciplinary conference on mental health had more influence than those representing lower-status groups (such as nurses, teachers, clergymen), independent of their actual contributions to the conference deliberations (see page 101). In children's groups, influence may be related to physical size, athletic skill, or fighting ability (Lippett *et al.*, 1952). Thus, even though a group explicitly assumes that all its members are equal in power (and both the jury and the interdisciplinary conference are predicated on that assumption), members may actually wield different degrees of power based on their general or specific statuses in the broader community within which the group exists.

3. COMMUNICATION STRUCTURE

A third basis for describing the structure of a group is in terms of the pattern of communication linkages among its members. A group's communication structure may be considered as the set of *possible* or *permissible* communication links or as the pattern of communication channels actually utilized during group activity. Here again, it is possible to focus on the communication properties of a particular role (for example, how central it is in the group's communication network; how heavy the load of messages which arise at or are sent to that position); or on the over-all pattern of the group's communication net (how much it is centralized around one person; how many total communication links there are).

A number of experiments have shown that the communication structure of a group has important consequences for the group's task performance and for the members' morale or satisfaction. Most of these studies were conducted with small groups that had experimentally imposed restrictions on the communication links among members. (For further descriptions of studies of restricted communication nets, see Leavitt, 1951; Bavelas, 1950; Guetzkow & Simon, 1955; Shaw, 1954; and a review by Glanzer & Glaser, 1961). The logic of these communication-net studies is as follows. If we restrict the potential communication channels within a group (if we permit each member to communicate only with certain other members), the actual flow of communications will necessarily be restricted. How will differences in flow of communication affect the group's task performance and the reactions of the members to the situation?

Most communication-net studies have been done with four- or five-man groups. Only certain pairs of members were permitted to communicate with each other, some of the potential channels being eliminated by experimental arrangements. The method of communication was restricted either to written notes or to non-face-to-face verbal communication over an intercom system. The open channels were usually two-way, permitting feedback. Sometimes limits were placed on the rate and the content of messages. The problems used always required an interchange of information; they sometimes required some problem-solving activities; they usually required feedback of information or solutions to other group members. The communication nets varied primarily in degree of centralization, that is, in how much they forced communication to be routed to one central person. Some typical communication nets studied in these experiments are shown in Figure 3.

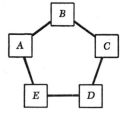

The circle, a decentralized communication network in which all members are equally central

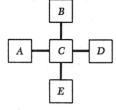

The wheel, a centralized communication network in which position *C* is central and all others are peripheral

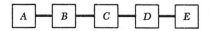

The chain, a moderately centralized communication network in which position *C* is central, positions *B* and *D* are intermediate, and positions *A* and *E* are peripheral

FIGURE 3 Diagram of Some Communication Patterns Used in Studies of Groups with Experimentally Restricted Communication Networks. Boxes labeled *A, B, C, D,* and *E* represent positions; lines represent possible communication channels between persons in designated positions.

These studies show two major results:

a. For simple problems, centralized nets (such as the wheel and to a lesser degree the chain in Figure 3) produce faster and more accurate problem solving than less centralized nets (such as the circle in Figure 3). The leader (position *C* in the centralized nets in Figure 3) is happy in his central position but other group members are less satisfied. Individual satisfaction is directly related to the individual's centrality in the group (how near he is to the central person in terms of communication links).

b. For more complex problems, performance differences among nets tend to diminish. The effectiveness of highly centralized nets depends largely on the leader's ability and his utilization of members' skills. The relationship between member satisfaction and member centrality, however, tends to persist for the more complex problems.

Laboratory studies by Kelley (1951) and Thibaut (1950) have shown also that the frequency, direction, and content of actual communications in groups which had no externally imposed communication restrictions are related to the relative status of members and the likelihood that their status could change. In general, high-status members talked more than low-status members, and both high- and low-status members directed more communications to those with high status. When low-status members had no chance for upward status movement, they directed more communications to high-status persons and engaged in more task-irrelevant communications than did low-status members who had some possibility of an upward change in status. Presumably, upward communication in this instance served as a substitute for upward status movement. (Kelley's study is referred to again on page 100.)

4. FRIENDSHIP OR AFFECT STRUCTURE

There is at least one other general basis for description of group structure, namely, the friendship or affect pattern of a group. The affect structure has to do with patterns of relationships among group members as persons, rather than the relationships among roles. The member structure patterns, however, are highly interdependent with various dimensions of the group's role structure.

For one thing, there are fairly strong role expectations about what kind of affect relations ought to exist between persons in certain role relationships. For example, mothers "should" love their children; bosses "should" be friendly but retain a certain aloofness or businesslike attitude in relation to subordinates; soldiers "should" hate enemy soldiers; in some situations the worker is expected to be hostile toward the boss. For the most part, such expected affect relations between occupants of different positions actually become a part of the role relationship between them.

The communication pattern also influences (and is influenced by) the affect relations that develop between occupants of different positions. We seldom develop either positive or negative attitudes toward persons with whom we do not interact (except, of course, toward persons in positions for which our own position gives us an expected affect relation, for example, toward "an enemy"). We may, of course, develop strong attitudes toward public figures, such as political leaders. When we do, though, we often feel that we know them, even though we are aware that they do not have reciprocal attitudes.

In fact, Festinger and his associates (1950) have shown that mere proximity, which provides the opportunity to interact, is the most important factor in determining what friendship patterns arise between families within a housing development. That is, we develop friendships with those with whom we have occasion to interact. Conversely, Newcomb (1961) has shown that once a friendship pattern has been established, we tend to seek opportunities to interact with those we like and avoid interaction with those we dislike.

Affect relations show the same kind of interdependence with power relations. In all the studies of effects of power or status which we have cited (Strodtbeck *et al.*, 1957; Hurwitz *et al.*, 1960; Lippett *et al.*, 1952; Kelley, 1951; Thibaut, 1950), persons with high status not only received more deference but also were more popular. We tend to be attracted to people who occupy positions of high power. Of course, this tendency depends on the form or basis of that power; it probably does not hold for power based on coercion, for example. Conversely, we tend to influence and be influenced by those we like. Back (1951) has shown that two-person groups whose members like one another exhibit more attempted influence and more often succeed in these attempts, than groups whose member do not like one another. The tendency to be influenced by those we like may account for the rule in many work organizations which forbids nepotism (employment of two or more persons who are related by blood or marriage). Role relations on the job are expected to be affectively neutral; while role relations among kinfolk are expected to include positive affect. We therefore expect (and indeed often find) that the juxtaposition of these two kinds of role relations within the same role system may have disruptive effects.

We can consider the over-all pattern of affect relations in a group, as well as the affect ties of a particular member. Groups vary in terms of the extent to which the pattern of affect relationships among members tends to partition the group into separate subgroups or cliques, and in terms of whether there is active hostility or just lack of positive relations between members of one clique and another. Interaction cliques tend to become affect cliques, and vice versa. Such divisions within a group may or may not correspond with task-based subgroupings. The presence of antagonistic cliques in a group detracts from the efficiency of group-task performance, at least when the task requires close coordination between persons in the different cliques.

Similarly, we can consider the effects of the over-all level of positive or negative affect relations in a group. Much has been written about the importance of good interpersonal relations in work groups, most of it on the assumption that groups whose members like one another perform their tasks better. Actually, there is little research evidence on the connection between interpersonal relations and task effectiveness, and what evidence does exist is not at all clear-cut. It does seem clear that negative affect relations within a group disrupt group performance; it does not necessarily follow, however, that positive affect relations facilitate group performance.

Too much friendship within a work group can result in the group's spending most of its time on social activities rather than on the task. Even when a group with highly positive interpersonal relations does concentrate on task activities, there is no guarantee that it will do so effectively. When a group does have positive interpersonal relations among its members, though, there is at least some assurance that the group's task performance will not be hindered by the disruptive effects of negative interpersonal relations, and the group's task performance will depend more closely on the skills and abilities of its members and on the extent to which its task and communication structures facilitate (or hinder) task performance.

Although positive interpersonal relations among members do not necessarily lead to group task success, task success does seem to lead to an increase in positive affect relations among group members. Thus, we tend to like those who have helped us gain rewards.

This discussion is related to a structure problem that can have serious consequences for members of formal work organizations; namely, the problem of the "fit" between the affect structure of the group and its formal work, authority, and communication structures. Formal organizations usually spell out task responsibilities and power relations among members. Usually they also specify preferred or required communication relations among members (and, by implication, those possible communication linkages that are not supposed to be used), at least regarding the communication of task-relevant and organization-relevant information. These structure patterns are often embodied in a formal organization chart. Within such formal organizations, informal friendship groups often develop. These are likely to have informal communication structures, utilized primarily for nontask communications. The informal communication pattern may or may not conflict with the formal pattern of communication as prescribed in the organization chart.

An individual member is likely to have a position and a set of roles in both the formal and informal structures. In certain situations role expectations for his behavior may be divergent and mutually exclusive. Thus, the individual may be placed in a role-conflict situation. Resolution of such role conflicts depends on the relative attraction of the member to the formal and informal groups, which in turn depends upon how well these groups satisfy his various needs and aspirations. The formal organization may largely control the satisfaction of certain of the individual's goals, such as economic gain or occupational status. The informal group is likely to be the main instrument for satisfaction of other goals, such as recognition, prestige, friendship. Resolution of such role conflicts often requires the individual to choose between a number of important and separate goals or compromise. We will discuss this and other forms of role-performance conflicts again in Chapter 11.

CHAPTER 9

| *Leadership*

Historically, the subject of leadership has been considered a separate and important topic of social psychology, and much research effort has been devoted to it. The basic questions pursued in this area have been: What makes a good leader? How can leaders be distinguished from nonleaders? How can effective leaders be distinguished from ineffective leaders? How can good leaders be identified and selected? How can men be trained to become good leaders? The impetus behind the extensive research on leadership seems to have been due more to the tremendous practical importance of being able to select and train effective leaders than to the theoretical importance of the questions or the rate of progress which has been made on the problem.

The trait approach

Much early research on leadership, as well as much current work, has been based on a "trait" theory of leadership. Such an approach attempts to identify those characteristics of the leader which are associated with group effectiveness. The trait approach to leadership like the search for meaningful group properties, has been remarkably unsuccessful. Except for fairly consistent but small relationships of effective leadership with general intelligence and other measures of competence, this approach has generally failed to identify a set of characteristics which are consistently associated with effective leadership.

Several reasons may account for the lack of success of the trait approach to leadership. First, there is no agreed upon set of important personal or personality traits which can serve as anchors for such studies. Nor has there been much agreement on a definition of "leader." The leader of a group has been defined in some studies as the man who is formally assigned as leader by an outside authority. In other studies, the leader has been defined in terms of popularity (the person most liked by other group members), in terms of opinion leadership (the person who most influences others in the group), or in terms of amount of participation. It is little wonder that studies using different definitions of leadership and different measures of leader attributes have yielded results that are not consistent.

Such definitions of leader are conceptually distinct because they differ in terms of the basis upon which the leader holds power. There is certainly a vast difference in the basis of power (hence, in the leader's relationships with other group members) for a self-appointed leader who has emerged in an unstructured situation, a leader who has been elected to the role by the group, and a leader who has been appointed to office by some authority outside of and superordinate to the group.

The trait approach encounters difficulty also because it requires that the group led by a given individual (leader) be effective in performance of its task regardless of the characteristics of other members of the group, the nature of the task, or the environmental conditions under which the group operates. Many theorists have argued, with considerable force, that successful leadership of a group depends as much on the followers as on the leader. Others have proposed that leadership is situationally determined, that is, that characteristics of the task and situation largely determined which group member would be most effective as leader of the group.

As a further difficulty, the trait approach requires that each group have a single leader. Everyday observations make it apparent that groups often have different leaders in different situations. For example, in the average United States family it is likely that the father is leader (that is, he has most influence and makes final decisions) in a number of matters such as the family's place of residence and major expenditures. In many other situations, though, the mother may well be leader; she has most influence and makes final decisions in such matters as behavior rules for the children, furnishings and decoration of the house, and meals for the family. It may be that in other areas of family life there is no clear leader; the father, mother, and children may all share equally in leading some of the family activities. Similar illustrations can be made for many other types of formal and informal groups.

Recent research on small groups supports the idea that some groups have multiple leaders, each specialized as to function, at one and the same time. Laboratory experiments by Bales and Slater (1955) suggest that groups engaged in problem-solving tasks tend to develop two types of leaders: one specialized in task leadership, the other specialized in the resolution of social-emotional problems. Hutchins and Fiedler (1960) obtained similar results for military and college dormitory groups. Hence, the search for a formal definition that will permit identification of a single leader in each group may not only be difficult to handle from a theoretical point of view but also out of keeping with circumstances in real-life groups.

Two main conclusions can be drawn from these considerations. First, many classes of variables affect group task performance. The characteristics of any particular member (the leader) may play a part, but characteristics of the group, its task and environment, and the on-going group process also affect the group's task performance. Thus, it would seem extremely unlikely that the group's task effectiveness could be predicted to a very high degree on the basis of any one or a few characteristics of one member (the leader). Hence, it seems more useful to shift ground from concern with the traits of the leader to concern with the complex interactions of leader, members, and situation.

Secondly, it seems clear that what we intend to mean by leadership refers to the performance of certain role behaviors rather than to the occupant of a certain role. Furthermore, these leadership behaviors may be concentrated in one man (the leader) or distributed over several or even all members of the group. If leader behavior is carried out by members as well as by a nominal leader, the leader-trait approach is largely inapplicable.

Leadership-effectiveness traits

While the trend today is away from study of the characteristics of the leader and toward study of leadership as an interaction of leader, group, and situation, one major exception to this trend has been in Fiedler's (1961) research on leadership-effectiveness traits.

Fiedler's rationale is based on two salient criticisms of much of the earlier work on leadership traits. First, much of that research concentrated on identifying differences between leaders and nonleaders. At best this approach yields information only about individuals who attain nominal positions of leadership; it does not say anything about how effective those individuals are in their leadership roles. People may become nominal leaders for a variety of reasons, including such irrelevant ones as nepotism, seniority, and historical accident. Hence, it is not likely that we will find systematic differences between the class of persons who hold nominal leadership roles and the class of persons who do not hold such roles. Nor would we have learned very much about leadership, in more fundamental senses, if we did find such differences.

Furthermore, Fiedler argues, when we identify an individual as nominal leader of a group (often via appointment by authorities external to that group), we have not necessarily identified an individual who is notably central to the group in terms of influence on the behavior of other group members. Often, such individuals are leaders in name without being leaders in fact.

To test the trait approach properly in the leadership field, Fiedler maintains, research must meet at least two important conditions. First, it must deal with leadership-effectiveness traits. It must focus on a search for characteristics that differentiate effective leaders from ineffective leaders rather than seek traits that differentiate leaders (good or poor) from those who do not hold leadership roles. For Fiedler, the effectiveness of the leader is to be assessed primarily in terms of the group's task-performance effectiveness.

Fiedler's second requirement is that research focus on the study of leaders in fact rather than leaders in name only. Thus, an individual must not only be the occupant of a formally defined leadership role, but also be accepted in that role by at least his key subordinates in order for him to have a meaningful impact on the group's performance.

Much of Fiedler's own work has been in pursuit of such leadership-effectiveness traits. He has found that leaders who have certain types of interpersonal attitudes toward coworkers *and* are accepted by their key subordinates have more effective groups than leaders who do not meet both these conditions. The interpersonal attitudes involved are those having to do with the leader's perceptions of the personality characteristics of his most preferred and least preferred coworkers. Leaders who perceive large differences in personality traits between their most and least preferred coworkers are said to *assume little similarity between opposites*. In Fiedler's terms, they have low ASo scores. These low ASo leaders (provided they have positive affect relationships with key subordinates) tend to have more effective groups than leaders with high ASo scores (leaders who tend to perceive relatively little difference in personality between their most and least preferred coworkers).

Fiedler's basic finding is that leaders who are accepted by their key men (and hence are leaders in fact) *and* who have low ASo scores have more effective groups than high ASo leaders. This finding has been confirmed in a series of field studies conducted with basketball teams, student surveying crews, steel mill work crews, Air Force bomber crews, and Army tank crews (Fiedler, 1958). Fiedler interprets the low ASo score as reflecting a strong task orientation on the part of the leader, indicating that he accepts or rejects (rewards or punishes) coworkers primarily on the basis of their task competence and task performance (Fiedler, 1961). These studies suggest that the ASo score of the leader-in-fact seems to be a measure of a leadership-effectiveness trait.

However, in some recent laboratory experiments, Fiedler and his coworkers have obtained additional findings which seem to require that the leadership-effectiveness trait conception be qualified in terms of differences in situational factors (Fiedler, 1962). In three separate studies of experimentally created groups engaged in tasks calling for joint creative efforts, Fiedler found no over-all relationship between leader ASo scores (or their major component, the favorableness of leader perceptions of the least preferred coworker) and group-creativity scores. When groups were further divided into those in which the leader perceived the group as having a relatively pleasant and relaxed atmosphere and those in which the leader perceived the group atmosphere as unpleasant and tense, certain more complicated relationships were revealed. In groups where the leader perceived a pleasant group atmosphere, leaders with high ASo scores had more successful groups. This is directly opposite to earlier findings. However, in groups where the leader perceived a relatively unpleasant group atmosphere, the low ASo leader had the more effective, creative groups.

Fiedler has extended his earlier interpretations to take into account the interactive effects of the situation on the relationship between leader style and group effectiveness. He holds that under relatively pleasant group atmosphere conditions, the controlling and managing nature of the low ASo leader's style is unnecessary and may even be objectionable to group members who are already under conditions likely to foster maximum creative efforts. Hence, it is the high ASo leader, with his more easy-going, person-oriented style, whose groups achieve greatest success on the task. In less pleasant groups, however, the task-oriented style of the low ASo leader is apparently required or at least useful in aiding the group to achieve maximum creative effort.

It should also be noted that Fiedler's research encompasses a number of different tasks and differences in various membership and group structural properties, as well as differences in perceived situational stress. For example, the earlier studies of problem-solving groups (Fiedler, 1958), in which the original ASo findings were obtained, were done as field studies in natural settings and involved subject groups that varied widely in terms of such factors as age, education level, and occupation. The more recent studies of creativity in groups (Fiedler, 1962), which led to the modifications of the original hypothesis, were done under laboratory conditions on artificially created groups, most of whom were in the upper levels of education and intelligence. These factors, too, may modify the effect of leader style on group task performance. That is, the leader who is effective in one type of group on a given type of task and in a given situational context may or may not be effective when placed (1) with a different group, (2) with the same group but on a different task, or (3) with the same group on the same task but under different environmental conditions. Thus, Fiedler's leadership-effectiveness trait approach has also come to center on the *interaction of leader, group, task, and situation,* supporting the dominant trend in current leadership research.

Leadership as role behavior

If we are no longer to be concerned with study of the leader but are to shift our attention to the study of leadership behavior, we are immediately faced with a new definitional problem. What forms of behavior are to be considered leadership behavior? Those who have followed the leadership-behavior approach have developed a variety of answers to this question. These have varied from the broad definition of leadership behavior as influence, to much more delimited statements of the key functions of leadership as distinguished from other group behavior.

1. LEADERSHIP AS INFLUENCE

The most broadly defined concept of leadership equates it with the process of interpersonal influence. Formulations by Back (1961), French (1956), J. R. Gibb (1961), and others imply such a definition of leadership.

Back's formulation distinguishes between the concepts of power, influence, and authority. He holds that a person has *power* (is a leader) to the extent that he can alter the attitudes and/or the behavior of others. He terms the leader's effects on member attitudes as *influence* and his effects on member behavior as *authority.* He then provides a formal model that explains why attitude change and behavior change are often uncorrelated.

Back's formulation is related to French's theory of social power (French,

1956; French & Raven, 1959). While Back is concerned with the inter-personal process (communication) by which a given individual wields power (influence or authority) within a group, French and Raven deal with the various sources from which an individual may derive his power in a group. They specify five main sources: expertness, possibility of reward, possibility of coercion, attraction, and legitimacy. Back sees the first three of these bases of power as relevant to the exercise of authority (that is, the changing of actions without necessarily changing attitudes). He sees the fourth source of power, attraction, as most relevant to influence (that is, changes in attitudes). The fifth source, legitimacy, may affect both influence and authority.

Putting these two points of view together, then, we can think of the leadership or interpersonal-influence process as the application of one or more of five distinct sources of power, in any of a variety of patterns of interpersonal communication, toward the attainment of either or both of two kinds of effects: influence (change of attitude) and/or authority (change of action). Obviously, leadership in the usual sense of the word is concerned with the attainment of both attitudinal (long-run) and action (short-run) effects.

2. LEADERSHIP AS INITIATION OF STRUCTURE

Several recent theoretical positions define leadership as initiation of structure. This is a somewhat more specific definition of leadership behavior than the view that leadership equals influence. Hemphill (1961) who is a leading protagonist of this view, defines leadership behavior as referring to all of those actions intended to "initiate a structure in the interaction of others, as part of a process of solving a mutual problem." Leaders, then, are to be identified in terms of the relative frequency with which they engage in actions that attempt to shape the behavior of others in the group.

This formulation has several important advantages. First, such a definition delimits the meaning of leadership behavior much more than the influence approach and begins to denote something much closer to the usual lay meaning of leadership. More important, this view permits multiple leaders, or for that matter no leader at all, within any given group. In fact, Hemphill's conception of leadership behavior blends nicely with the notion that every group member is more or less a leader. It permits measurement of the degree of leadership behavior exhibited by every member of a given group or organization. Thus it offers an opportunity to explore the correlates of frequency of attempts to lead.

This concept of leadership leads Hemphill to distinguish between three phases of leadership activity: attempted leadership, successful leadership, and effective leadership (Hemphill, 1961). Attempted leadership refers to the frequency with which an individual exhibits acts that are intended (by the experimenter's inference) to initiate structure in the interactions of other group members. Successful leadership refers to the relative frequency with which a given individual's attempts to lead do in fact alter the structure-in-interaction of others. The effectiveness of leadership refers to how much a given member's successful attempts to lead aid the group in solution of the task in which it is engaged. The latter is clearly related to the leadership-effectiveness notion espoused by Fiedler (1961). Further, it permits a definition of the leadership effectiveness of every member of the group, whereas Fiedler focused mainly on a single person as leader. Hemphill's intermediate concept of leadership success appears to be a more rigorous formulation of Fiedler's notion that we must study leaders-in-fact, rather than nominal leaders if we are to make major progress toward an understanding of leadership phenomena.

3. THE LEADER AS COMPLETER OF ESSENTIAL GROUP FUNCTIONS

Another set of theoretical formulations of the leadership role can best be characterized as approaches that view the leader as the completer of essential group functions. The term "completer" is used by Schutz (1961) to describe the key function of the leader. Roby (1961) has a similar formulation in which he designates the key function of leader as "the ability to fill any breach in the executive process." Roby sees such versatility as more important than any particular function which the leader may perform on a routine basis. Berrien (1961), in a similar formulation, states that the most important task of the leader is to maintain a balance between group need satisfaction and formal achievement on the task.

These three formulations build on the concept of a set of critical group functions which define the important needs and activities of the group and which apply to any group in any situation. Schutz, Roby, and Berrien each describe these critical group functions within his own terms of reference. Each then posits that the proper role of the leader is to insure that *all* of the group's critical functions are adequately fulfilled and that a proper balance is maintained among them.

A leader may carry out his essential function if, having noted a deficiency in group performance of a critical function, he himself performs the necessary activity. Such leaping into the breach for a group deficiency, however, must be thought of as basically a stopgap measure. The fundamental task of the leader is to become aware of such deficiencies in critical group functions and to institute activities (by himself or by others) which will reduce that deficiency.

This view of the leader as completer ties in closely with the conceptualization of the leader as initiator of structure in interaction. Rather than defining leadership in terms of the relative frequency of acts which initiate structure, as do Hemphill and others, the leader-as-completer approach views initiation of structure in interaction as the appropriate leader response *when* he has diagnosed a deficiency in the group's attainment of one or more of its critical functions.

The crucial problem for proponents of this position, of course, is the need to establish a set of critical group functions which will be sufficiently general to apply to all groups under a wide range of conditions. Both Roby (1961) and Schutz (1961) have attempted such formulations, the former emphasizing critical task functions and the latter emphasizing interpersonal relations and the individual needs of members. While the problem of defining leadership behavior, and/or critical group functions, is as yet far from solved, the general approach that studies leadership as role behavior seems to offer promise for gaining understanding of leadership phenomena.

CHAPTER 10

/ *Group interaction*
process

The frame of reference, we are using for analysis of group phenomena (see Figure 2, page 70) carries the implied assumption that whenever a variable from one of the classes of antecedent conditions (member, group, or task characteristics) is related to a variable in one of the classes of consequent conditions (effects on member, group, or task) the relationship is mediated via the interaction process. That is, for an individual variable or a group variable to have an effect, it must somehow be manifested in an interactional context. For example, the logic of the studies of effects of restricted communication nets on task performance and satisfaction in groups contains the premise that restriction of the communication net (a group-structure variable) does in fact lead to a parallel restriction of the flow of communication (a group-process variable) within the group.

Actually, relatively little research has been done directly on the question of how group interaction mediates member, group, and task effects. Most small group research has ignored interaction process. Of the research that has dealt with group interaction, much has attempted either to identify the determinants of particular patterns of interaction or to trace the consequences of different interaction patterns.

This chapter presents first a brief overview of the nature of interaction. Then we will consider various methods that have been developed for systematic observation and analysis of group interaction. Finally, we will review some studies of regularities in the group interaction process and conditions related to them.

Basic elements of the interaction process

We can view group interaction as including three elementary processes: communication, the flow of influence, and the flow of affect. Communication, the flow of meanings, is the process by which the group assembles its task resources and performs its tasks. The flow of influence is the process by which the group reaches decisions, sets goals, directs its activities. The flow of affect, positive and negative, is the process by which group members reward and punish one another and by which the group maintains (or fails to maintain) its solidarity.

These three processes operate in all group-interaction situations, although they vary in importance and in prominence from one situation to another. This does not mean, of course, that all these processes operate because of the deliberate, conscious intentions of group members.

Although these three processes can be distinguished conceptually, they are closely interrelated as they operate in interaction. Communication is a necessary precondition for influence to occur, or for positive or negative affect to be displayed. However, we are more likely to communicate with those toward whom we have positive feeling and with persons of high influence or status. We are also more likely to be influenced by those we like and to like those who have influence (persons of high status).

We have already discussed components of group structure which are related to these three processes: the communication network, the power structure, and the friendship or affect structure. The fourth aspect of group structure, the division of task activity, would imply a fourth aspect of the interaction process, namely, the flow of work. Much of the activity involved in the flow of work, however, is either interpersonal communication (which we will treat under the communication process), or behavior in reference to impersonal objects and not interpersonal interaction as such. Thus, we will not treat the flow of work as a separate facet of the interpersonal interaction process, though we must remember that much that we will say about the other facets of interaction often takes place within a work or task-activity context.

A group's structure (the pattern of relationships among members and/or roles) and its interaction process (the flow of events during group activity) are interdependent. Each of the aspects of group structure develops out of its parallel interaction process and tends to pattern that process subsequently. For example, Festinger *et al.* (1950) showed that the flow of communication in a housing development was initially based on proximity, or opportunity to communicate. This led to a systematic patterning of who communicated to whom, which we can consider the group's communication structure. This structure operated, subsequently, to limit or channel the flow of communication within the group.

Systems for measuring interaction

Quite a variety of methods for recording group inter-action have been developed. They vary in "depth," from some that are highly objective but yield somewhat superficial descriptions of group process, to others that require the observer to make depth inferences. They also vary in terms of whether they deal with the manifest content of the messages being communicated, the functional meanings of the message within the group-task context, or the underlying meaning of the message from the point of view of the actor. We will discuss five general types of systems for measuring the interaction process.

1. *Systems that deal with form rather than content* (for example, Chapple, 1940). Systems of this type are concerned with descriptive properties of the communication, using indices such as total number of messages by each person, total communication time per person, frequency of usage of various word forms or phrases, frequency of use of any one communication link. Such systems have the advantages of extreme objectivity and high reliability. They overlook distinctions based on the content of the interaction.

2. *Systems that use content classifications.* For example, Carter *et al.* (1951) classified each verbal act into one of about fifty categories such as: calls for attention, asks for information, diagnoses situation, initiates action, supports his proposal, argues with others, offers to help. Such systems deal with the manifest content of each act, requiring little inference on the part of the observers. They have the disadvantage of an extremely large number of categories, often more categories than acts to be classified.

3. *Systems based on the function of the act for the group.* The primary example of this type is the system developed by Bales (1950), which uses a relatively small number of categories (twelve) that are related to one another in a tight classification schema. The Bales system is discussed in more detail below.

4. *Systems based on the intention of the act, or the individual's motivation in performing the act.* For example, the system used by Fouriezos,

Hutt, and Guetzkow (1950) used categories such as: dependency, status, dominance, aggression, catharsis.

5. *Systems based on latent personality processes* (for example, Thelen, 1950). An even greater degree of inference is required for such systems than for those based on the intention of the act. Their basic categories are personality characteristics such as: tendencies to flight-fight, tendencies toward dependence, tendencies toward pairing. These systems interpret interactions as expressions of the individual's underlying personality.

Perhaps the most thoroughly developed and most widely used system for recording interaction is that of Bales (1950), which is based on the function of the act for the group. In this system, each meaningful act or unit of speech is classified separately. A record is kept of who speaks to whom, in a temporal sequence, each act being classified into one and only one of twelve categories: (1) shows solidarity, (2) shows tension release, (3) shows agreement, (4) gives suggestion, (5) gives opinion, (6) gives information, (7) asks information, (8) asks opinion, (9) asks suggestion, (10) shows disagreement, (11) shows tension, (12) shows antagonism.

The twelve categories can be divided into four classes: active-task contributions (4, 5, and 6) and passive-task contributions (7, 8, and 9); and positive socio-emotional contributions (1, 2, and 3) and negative socio-emotional contributions (10, 11, and 12). Thus three categories fall within each of the four classes. The system can be used to develop total and relative participation measures for the whole set of categories, for each category, or for any subset of categories. It can also be used to develop profiles, by person or by group, for an entire session or for any time segment of it.

Some studies of group interaction

The group interaction process is by no means a random pattern or a process that is unique to each group in each situation. There are some fairly general regularities in the pattern of interaction by which members of groups relate to one another. For example, Bales has used his system for recording interaction to generate and test a "problem-solving phase sequence" hypothesis (Bales & Strodtbeck, 1951). This hypothesis states that in problem-solving groups there is a fixed sequence of phases in the group's activity, namely, an orientation phase, an evaluation phase, and a control or decision phase. The relative use of any interaction category will reach a peak at the point where its problem-solving phase is being dealt with. Thus, for example, category 6, "gives information" (orientation phase) will be at a peak in the first time portion of a group problem-solving session, while category 5 "gives opinion" (evaluation) will reach its peak somewhat later. The relative amount of socio-emotional communication, both positive and negative, will increase as the group goes through successive stages of the problem-solving process. This hypothesis appears to hold for a wide range of types of groups working on a variety of group problems.

Analysis of interaction has been used in several studies (Bales & Slater, 1955) to investigate the differentiation of roles in unstructured problem-solving groups. These studies generally find that three relatively distinct and specialized functions tend to be differentiated in such groups, with different members "specializing" in each of the three functions. The first function is that of task leader or problem-solving specialist. (There may be two forms of task-leader role, the "idea man" and the process leader, though these tend to be highly correlated.) The second function is that of group harmonizer, or the group's social-emotional specialist. These specialized functions are seldom performed by the same person, especially if group interaction is prolonged beyond an initial brief session. The third function, which is sometimes differentiated and sometimes not, is that of high participater. Sometimes the highest participater is the same person as the idea man. Seldom is he the same person as the social-emotional specialist. Often the highest participater is a member other than either the task leader or the social-emotional specialist. The task leader and the social-emotional specialist tend to form a strong mutually supportive alliance, at least in groups that develop a stable role structure. They tend to communicate with each other more than with any other group member and to like each other more than other members. When the two top men do not form such an alliance, they may challenge each other's status in the group, this sometimes leading to a redistribution of roles and to disruption of group activities.

A number of studies have illustrated that characteristics of individual members, of the group's structure, and of the group's situation (its task and environment) partly determine the group's pattern of interaction. For example, in several studies the power or status of the members has been shown to affect the rate, direction, and nature of interaction.

Kelley (1951) conducted an experiment in which all participants actually had the same task, but some subjects were told that theirs was a relatively high-status job, while other subjects were told that "the other member" had the high-status job. Within each of these conditions, some participants were told that they would not change jobs during the experiment, while others were told that they might be changed depending on their performance. Communication was permitted only by written notes, which were intercepted by the investigator and used as data. Results showed that high-status members communicated more than low-status members. Both directed more of their communications to high-status persons. Highs were not critical of their own role when communicating with lows, though they were critical of the role performance of lows. Lows, especially the potentially mobile lows, were not critical of highs. Lows, especially the nonmobile lows, communicated more task-irrelevant messages.

In a related study Strodtbeck *et al.* (1957) examined the effects of socioeconomic status of jurors on their leadership, participation, and influence. He played recorded court cases to mock juries, recorded their interaction, and obtained information on personal characteristics of jurors and on their individual reactions to jurymates and to the situation. Results showed that socioeconomically high-status jurors and males (1) were significantly more likely to be chosen chairman, (2) had higher relative participation and higher influence on other jurors, and (3) were more likely to be preferred by other jurors.

These findings were confirmed in a study by Hurwitz *et al.* (1960). They studied interaction in mental health conferences composed of psychiatrists, psychologists, teachers, nurses, doctors, and others to examine the effects of the differential status of professions on interaction behavior and influence. In short, they asked: Does the pattern of interaction in interdisciplinary conferences depend on the relative status of the professions of the participants? They obtained premeasures of esteem and post-conference personal reactions. The results jibe with Kelley's and with Strodtbeck's findings. Persons in high-status professions talked more, were more often addressed by others, were more often critical, and were less often criticized.

Little research evidence exists on the relation between group interaction and group task performance. What is available suggests that groups which are successful on their tasks exhibit less negative affect (hostility) than groups which are not as successful, though they do not necessarily exhibit more positive affect (friendliness). Task performance does not seem to be related to total amount of interaction. The evidence about relations between task performance and other aspects of interaction is unclear.

CHAPTER 11

/ Member, group, and task effects

The interplay of group composition, structure, and task variables within the group interaction process leads to several kinds of consequences or outcomes. First, there are outcomes that have to do with the group's efforts to reach its goals; we will call these task-performance effects. Secondly, group activity may lead to changes in the group itself, such as development and changes of group norms and modifications of group structure, which we will call group-development effects. Finally, groups may produce effects on their members, including changes in attitudes, conforming behavior, conflicts related to role performance.

We have already considered some of these effects in our discussions of group composition, structure, and process. For example, we noted effects of various communication nets on both task performance and member morale. In this chapter, we shall review these effects and note some additional effects of group interaction on task performance, group development, and group members. Then we shall discuss the relation among these different effects, notably, the relation between individual satisfaction, interpersonal relations, and task performance.

Task performance

Investigation of factors which affect group task perform-ance has been, in a sense, the heart of small group research. Since the earliest studies of groups, measures of many member, group, and task variables have been related to the effectiveness of group task performance. These studies have in general shown a fairly consistent pattern although results obtained from laboratory experiments tend to be much more clear-cut than results from field studies. Over-all, the available evidence seems to support several general propositions.

First, given certain other conditions, the higher the level of both gen-eral and task-specific abilities of group members and the more training and practice they have on the task, the higher is the level of task-perform-ance effectiveness. This proposition is certainly not very surprising, and may even seem trivial. It should probably be treated as a baseline propo-sition that holds only under certain conditions. In fact, Steiner and Raja-ratnam (1961) suggest that member abilities represent an *upper limit* of potential group performance, while various individual factors (such as level of motivation) and group factors (such as coordination) are likely to reduce the *actual* level of task performance exhibited by the group. Thus, abilities and task experience determine task success to the extent that other conditions do not operate to reduce task-performance effective-ness.

Task performance depends also on the size of the group and the nature of its task. We noted above that early studies of coacting groups found problem-solving better for individuals working together than for indi-viduals working alone. The *reverse* relationship (that is, individuals work-ing alone do better than individuals working in the presence of others) holds for tasks requiring manual performance. We also noted that task performance was better (there were fewer errors) for *interacting* groups than for individuals working alone on intellectual tasks of a problem-solving type (Taylor & Faust, 1952). This finding has been used as a justification for the new management technique called brainstorming, which uses groups rather than individuals to try to develop new and creative ideas. However, Taylor *et al.* (1957) have shown that groups are inferior to individuals, in both quality and quantity, for creativity tasks requiring the generation of original or creative ideas. Thus, the use of groups rather than individuals to "brainstorm" creative ideas probably reduces task effectiveness.

We have already noted that highly centralized communication nets tend to give better task performance for simple information-handling tasks. A number of studies have shown that for more complex tasks centralized communication nets lose their advantage. In fact, for relatively complex tasks, the evenness of distribution of task-relevant information and its immediate accessibility to the group seem to affect task effectiveness more than the group's communication network as such.

Group task performance is also greatly affected by the reward conditions of the task. Groups perform better as groups when they are rewarded as groups than when performance results in differential rewards to different members (for example, Deutsch, 1949; Mintz, 1951). Thus, operating conditions that foster cooperative rather than competitive behavior among group members promote task effectiveness. It has been shown, too (Fouriezos, Hutt, & Guetzkow, 1950), that group task performance is disrupted if members focus their energies on fulfillment of self-needs (such as aggression, catharsis, dependence, status) rather than on the achievement of group goals.

We have noted that the relationship between group composition and task performance is unclear, except for the generalization about the favorable effects of high levels of ability. However, it does seem that task performance is better when group members have a range of skills, similar backgrounds and attitudes, and patterns of personality which are compatible and not too extreme.

We saw earlier that there is relatively little evidence which ties down specific relationships between aspects of group process and effectiveness of task performance. One major exception is the consistent finding that groups which are effective in their tasks have less negative interpersonal behavior than ineffective groups. There is little evidence that they interact either more or less, or that they have more behavior indicating positive interpersonal affect. These results suggest that successful groups may show less negative affect because they show more "affect neutrality" in their interpersonal interaction. They are less hostile and more task-oriented and "businesslike," but members are neither more nor less friendly toward one another.

Group development

While differentiation of roles often begins very quickly when a new group is formed, role differentiation and group structure continue to develop and change as the group continues its history. Such change generally diminishes through time, however, and group structure tends to stabilize, provided there is reasonable stability in the group's environment. For example, Newcomb (1961) found that the communication, influence, and affect structures within a university men's residence changed substantially during the first few weeks of a semester but tended to reach a fairly stable pattern by the end of four or five weeks.

A major facet of group development that results from the interaction process is the development of group norms and pressures for conformity to those norms. These aspects of group development are fundamental to our understanding of how groups operate and how they influence members.

DEVELOPMENT OF GROUP NORMS

In the socialization of a child (or, in a sense, of any new member of a group), the individual learns to view relevant objects in the same frame of reference as do the significant persons in his world. He must do so in order to communicate with them about important objects and thus to get what he wants. This occurs in two ways: (1) the individual's perceptions are "corrected" when they differ from accepted perceptions and (2) the individual is exposed only to the shared frame of reference of the group. Thus, the individual learns to perceive the world in a way that is shared by the significant others around him.

Members of small face-to-face groups develop shared "ways of looking at the world" in much the same way that the individual does in the socialization process. These shared frames of reference are termed *norms*. Just as attitudes refer to the individual's predispositions to respond to a class of objects in a certain positive or negative way, so norms refer to shared predispositions of an interrelated set of people (a group) to respond to classes of objects in certain positive or negative ways. Group norms include: (1) the frame of reference in terms of which a given relevant object is viewed; (2) prescribed "right" attitudes or behavior toward that object; (3) affective feelings regarding the "rightness" (sacredness) of these attitudes and regarding violation of the norm; and (4) positive and negative sanctions by which proper behavior is rewarded or improper behavior is punished. Norms are "in the eye of the beholder." They exist for a given individual and influence his behavior to the extent that he *believes that relevant others hold those norms*, whether they actually do or not.

"Norm" is a generic term for group attitudes. Role expectations are one very special subclass of norms. They are norms about how group members should behave vis-à-vis one another. Norms develop about objects other than group members. Groups develop norms (that is, group members come to share beliefs and feelings) about many things: basic values; the relative desirability of occupations, food, and other material goods; man's relation to God and to the universe. Groups often develop norms about the goodness or badness of other groups and of members of those groups; such norms play a part in the formation of stereotypes and prejudices, which usually underlie intergroup hostility and conflict between racial, religious, class, occupational, and political groups.

PRESSURES FOR CONFORMITY

The description of the development of group norms implies that group members influence one another. To do so, they must interact via communication or the transmission of meanings.

When two or more individuals interact via communication, they co-orient to one another and to the content of the interaction. They necessarily develop shared meanings for symbols to some extent and a shared frame of reference concerning their interaction. This frame of reference includes the attitude of each toward the other(s), their attitudes toward objects relevant to the interaction, and the estimates, perception, or beliefs of each about the attitudes of the other(s) toward him and toward the objects of co-orientation. (See the discussion of Newcomb's theory about *A-B-X* systems, page 50.)

Such interpersonal co-orientation systems tend to establish equilibrium, as was seen in our discussion of Newcomb's theory. As interaction continues, information is transmitted among the interacting individuals. Other things being equal, such information tends to increase accuracy of knowledge about the attitudes of others. Because of the tendency for balance or equilibrium, communication that leads to awareness of disagreement tends to produce further communication aimed at influencing the attitudes of others.

The more there is disagreement about a relevant object, the more communication there will be to the members who deviate from the group consensus, intended to produce a change in their attitudes. If pressure toward change proves fruitless, the deviate may leave the group or be forced to leave it. Hence, the more a member is attracted to the group, the more likely he is to be responsive to group pressures toward conformity to group norms.

A study by Schachter (1951) illustrates some of these effects. Schachter studied group interaction with, and rejection of, a member who deviated from an important group norm. He asked: If one member deviates from a group norm, how will this affect the pattern of interaction and the subsequent pattern of group interpersonal relations? He assembled a series of groups, each group containing one member who was actually in league with the experimenter but who appeared to be a participating subject. The groups were required to reach a decision on a discussion problem.

The experimenter's confederate was instructed to take a position which deviated from that of the rest of the group. Measures of the amount of interaction and of post-session reactions to the deviate were obtained. Results: Communication to the deviate designed to change his position increased in direct relation to the degree of his deviation. If the group could not change him, it was likely to reject him.

Another example is a study by Back (1951) on the effects of group cohesiveness on group pressure to conform and on the amount of actual conformity by group members. He asked two-person groups (dyads) to write a joint story about a picture, but he had previously given the two group members slightly differing versions of the picture. He induced various types of high and low cohesiveness (strong or weak attraction of the members to the group) by experimental instructions. He measured amount of interaction, changes in attitudes, and post-session reactions. Results showed that high-cohesive groups, whatever the source or type of cohesiveness, tried to influence members more and achieved more influence than low-cohesive groups.

CONFORMITY TO GROUP NORMS

The description of the development of group norms and of pressures for conformity to those norms may seem to imply that the individual group member is at the mercy of group pressures and is highly likely to conform to whatever norms the group may establish. Furthermore, there has been much recent lament in the press and in quasi–social-science literature about the problem of too much conformity in our current society. Just how strong and pervasive is this tendency for the individual to conform to the group? And is such conformity necessarily bad, as is usually implied in popular writings on the topic? Since the question of conformity to group norms has aroused so much invective, we will discuss it in some detail, even though it is somewhat tangential to the material of the chapter.

First, *all* groups tend to establish common norms, that is, to develop a membership which shares beliefs and values about *relevant* things. Such shared beliefs are probably essential for the development or continuation of a group. Certainly some agreement in perception and meanings is essential so that group members may interact or communicate, and agreement on goals and/or means is essential so that group members may act in concert on any common task. This is certainly not a new phenomenon nor one unique to American society.

When members disagree on matters of central significance to the group, the preservation of group effectiveness, harmony, and intactness requires a resolution of the disagreement. Hence, pressures toward conformity, in the form of persuasive communication, are inevitable. This phenomenon, too, is neither new nor unique to our society.

The continued existence of a group depends on its ability to keep its members in effective interaction with one another. When disagreement occurs on matters vital to the group, such nonconformity may threaten the existence or effectiveness of the group. The power of a group to influence its members toward conformity with shared beliefs and actions depends on the positive and negative sanctions (rewards and punishments) the group has at its disposal. The influence of a group over its members depends on how strongly the members value their membership and its accompanying rewards (including interpersonal rewards such as recognition, status, and prestige as well as material rewards) and how much the members want to avoid the negative sanctions (social and physical punishments or expulsion from the group) which the group can impose.

Given that an individual deviates from an important group norm, any of several outcomes can ensue: First, he may persuade others to join his position and thus alter the group norm; or he may be persuaded to conform to the original norm. The higher his status (power) in the group, the more likely he is to change the attitudes of others and the less likely he is to change his own. If neither of these alternatives takes place, any of several others may occur. If he is free to leave the group and the group is of little importance to him, he may withdraw from it. Conversely, if he is of little importance to the group, he may be faced with the choice of conforming or being rejected by the group—or may even be rejected for the act of deviance whether or not he is willing to "recant." However, if he is of great importance to the group (if he is a high-status member in terms of power, popularity, or special skills), the group may tolerate the deviation in order to avoid the greater threat of loss of a key member.

Most individuals are enmeshed in a number of groups at any given time, and the norms of these groups are not likely to be in total accord. Where the norms of two groups to which the individual holds allegiance overlap and conflict, the individual is faced with a choice between them. Assuming for the moment that he has only two alternatives in a given instance, then no matter which alternative he chooses he is both conforming to the norms of one group and deviating from the norms of the other. Here the individual's choice will be affected by the *relative* power the two groups have to reward and/or punish him, by the relative importance of the disputed matter to the two groups, and by the relative power he has to influence the existing norms of the two groups.

Thus, the process of interpersonal influence is a fundamental and pervasive force in human affairs. But conformity of a deviating individual to the norms of a *particular* group is only one of its possible outcomes. It would be difficult to establish firm evidence as to whether there is more or less individual conformity to group norms now than in prior times, or in our society as compared with other societies. The greater part of the available evidence on this question comes from anthropological studies of primitive societies and from historical studies of our own society in earlier times. Most of it clearly implies that there was a great deal *more* conformity to traditions and customs of the group in the past than there is now, if we define conformity in terms of *uniformity of behavior and beliefs* among group members, regardless of whether the uniformity was by deliberate and conscious choice. However, if we insist on defining conformity as a conscious and deliberate "giving in" to group pressures, it is harder to make meaningful comparisons. The latter is so because one outstanding feature of earlier, more primitive cultures was the tremendous paucity *of choices available to the individual.*

In contrast, our current society is especially characterized by the wide range of choices which individuals are permitted *and required* to make. Hence, we now have far more opportunity to conform, in the sense of making conscious, deliberate choices that are in accord with social norms, precisely because we no longer unwittingly conform to a single prescribed set of beliefs and behaviors nearly so much as did our cultural ancestors. It is this phenomenon—a wide range of alternatives for individual choice in all areas of living—which is both new and especially characteristic of our society. If our deliberate choices are more often "conforming" choices, it may be largely because we make many more choices in our lives.

Effects on group members

The development of the individual is affected by membership in a group; this is a major reason for the study of groups. In Chapter 5, we discussed the Meadian hypothesis, which posits that our self-concept develops and changes as a function of the evaluation others make of us, and Newcomb's *A-B-X* model of interpersonal relations, which suggests that our attitudes are shaped by the attitudes of others whom we value. We have just completed a discussion of the related phenomenon of conformity. We mentioned earlier, in Chapter 7, that we evaluate ourselves and others by comparison of role behaviors with expectations for those behaviors and that such evaluations have consequences for the role occupant. We will now discuss these and related effects of groups on their members.

CONFLICTS ARISING FROM ROLE PERFORMANCE

We have already noted that people evaluate one another by comparing role expectation with role behavior and that our esteem for others depends on how well their behavior meets the requirements of their roles. The individual may encounter difficulty in several ways in adequately fulfilling his roles. First, little consensus may exist among persons in related roles on what behavior is appropriate for the occupant of a given role. This can occur either when the role is new and as yet undefined or when two or more sets of people have contrasting expectations for a given role. For example, a first-line supervisor in industry is likely to find himself in a role for which there are two different sets of expectations: those held by management and those held by the men he is supervising. Successful performance of his role requires that he meet the expectations of both groups. If the two sets of expectations are mutually incompatible, the supervisor cannot possibly succeed in the eyes of both groups.

A related kind of role difficulty can arise because of simultaneous relevance of multiple role relationships. A given individual is likely to be involved in several different role relationships in the same group or in several groups with overlapping membership. For example, the male head of a family is husband to his wife, father to his children, employee to his boss, supervisor to his subordinates, and colleague and friend to other sets of people. Usually we arrange our lives in a way that permits us to behave with respect to one role relationship at a time. Occasions arise, however, when two or more of our role relationships are operative at the same time. When this occurs, the individual may be faced with another kind of difficulty in role performance: if two different role relationships call for behaviors that are incompatible, the individual cannot adequately fulfill the expectations for both role relationships at the same time.

Killian (1952) has demonstrated this type of role-performance conflict in a study of reactions during the Texas City disaster. He found that men who did not have families located in the community were more effective in their performance of job-related safety functions than were men who were torn between their responsibilities to the company for disaster activities and their responsibilities for the safety of their families. Such conflicts arising from multiple role relationships occur often, in less dramatic form, in our everyday lives.

Even when the individual is operating in a single role and high consensus exists in expectations among people in related roles, he may still encounter role-performance difficulties because he perceives these expectations inaccurately. When we take on a new role, we must *learn* the role expectations for it. We often overlook inadequate role performance on the part of new group members; we recognize that they have to learn the ropes (learn their roles) before they can be expected to perform well.

An individual may perform a role poorly even though he perceives the expectations of others for the role clearly and accurately. This can occur because the individual is not motivated to perform the role so as to satisfy those expectations. Such role-based conflict may account in large part for the large discrepancy that often seems to exist between the behavior of adolescents in our society and the expectations their parents and other adults have for that behavior. Role performance may also fail to meet role expectations simply because the individual does not have sufficient ability to meet them. (The famous tale of Casey at the Bat is a perfect illustration of this kind of role-performance difficulty.)

Any of these types of failure to meet role expectations tend to lead to a reduction in esteem. Others evaluate us by comparing our role performances with their expectations. We evaluate ourselves by comparing our role behavior with our own expectations or standards; these are generally derived by an incorporation of the standards of others in related roles. Hence, this is one way in which our self evaluations are reflections of the evaluations others make of us. (See the discussion of George Mead's concepts in Chapter 5.)

INDIVIDUAL ADJUSTMENT

Many persons in fields related to the treatment of psychological disorders have suggested that certain kinds of group experiences can have a helpful effect on the adjustment of individual patients. Fiedler and associates (1959) have extended this notion to the study of presumably normal everyday work and living groups. Using both military and college populations, they found that individuals who perceived their associates to be similar to themselves and who were seen by others as similar (1) had better adjustment and (2) showed greater improvements in adjustment over several months, as compared with members of the same populations who did not perceive such similarities. A later study has shown that when perceptions of similarity are produced by experimental manipulation, they still lead to favorable effects on individual adjustment. From these and other findings, Fiedler has postulated that under certain conditions everyday work groups serve functions similar to that of the therapeutic situation; namely, they provide a medium that facilitates individual adjustment. He has termed these functions the "quasi-therapeutic" effects of work groups.

It is likely that the quasi-therapeutic character of a group depends on the particular members of the group and the group's situation. Myers (1962) found, for example, that both between-group competition and success on the task tended to have favorable effects on group cohesiveness and on the adjustment of individual members. A related study (McGrath, 1962a) showed that persons who tended to perceive one set of teammates as providing interpersonal support (as being quasi-therapeutic) tended to make the same judgments about a different set of teammates when they were reassembled into new groups. Hence, it may be that the therapeutic quality of some groups inheres, at least in part, in the "eye of the beholder." That is, the extent to which a group is quasi-therapeutic for its members may depend more on the tendencies of those members to perceive interpersonal support than on the overt behavior of group members toward one another.

The interaction of effects: Individual adjustment, interpersonal relations, and task performance

Is a group composed of happy, well-adjusted individuals who get along well with one another likely to be an effective group in terms of task performance? Much has been written on the relation between the quality of interpersonal relations and individual adjustment in groups, and the quality of task performance. It has often been implied that various kinds of group programs designed to improve group harmony and individual morale would also make the group and its members more effective on their tasks. Actually, there is very little solid evidence on the relationship between group harmony and individual morale, on the one hand, and group effectiveness, on the other. The data that do exist by no means give unqualified support to such a relationship.

For example, Schachter et al. (1951) conducted a study of productivity in cohesive and uncohesive groups. Cohesiveness was defined as the strength of member attraction to the group. Sources of such attraction can be liking for others, prestige of membership, or attractiveness of the group's task activities. Cohesive groups accepted more group pressure toward *either* a norm for higher productivity or a norm for lower productivity than did less cohesive groups. Thus, when cohesiveness is considered as the attraction to the group, the greater the cohesiveness the greater the power the group has to influence its members. Hence, cohesiveness is one of the determinants of productivity, because task success depends on the power of the group to influence members. However, the formal work organization is the one for which the productivity norm holds. The informal friendship group may be the one toward which members are attracted. If so, members of cohesive groups will be influenced toward the informal group's norm about productivity, be it high or low.

If the group tries to influence members toward high productivity, it will probably succeed. If the group tries to influence members toward low productivity, then cohesive groups will do poorly.

Some rather clear evidence indicates, however, that successful groups are more likely to have positive interpersonal relations than groups with a history of failure. These data suggest that success on the task *produces* favorable interpersonal relationships, rather than the other way around. There is some evidence, noted in the previous chapter, that negative interpersonal behavior (hostility) within a group is disruptive to group task performance. Perhaps the best summary comment on this problem is that while a happy group may or may not be effective, an unhappy group in which much interpersonal hostility is displayed will almost certainly be fairly ineffective in the long run.

Summary of the group

In Chapter 7, at the beginning of our consideration of groups, we presented a general framework for analysis of groups. We designated three classes of "input" variables which affect groups: member characteristics, group structure, and task and environmental characteristics. We noted, too, that the effects of these variables are manifested in the group interaction process and that group process can yield changes in variables of any of these three classes. This framework was presented in Figure 2, page 70.

Subsequent chapters considered a number of additional facets of group phenomena. These are listed in Figure 4, which presents the analytic framework in more detailed form and are summarized below.

We discussed four subclasses of characteristics that members bring with them to the group: abilities, attitudes, background characteristics (such as age and sex), and personality characteristics. We considered also how different levels of these member variables (such as different average ability of group members) and different patterns of these member variables (such as compatible personality patterns) affect the operation of groups (see group composition, in Chapter 8).

We introduced and discussed the group structural concepts of position, role, role relationship, role expectation, and role behavior, and dealt with group structure in terms of each of three dimensions along which a set of role relationships can be differentiated and integrated, namely, task activity, power, and communication. We considered also group structure in terms of the dimension of affect relationships among members, and discussed how the dimensions of group structure (task, power, communi-

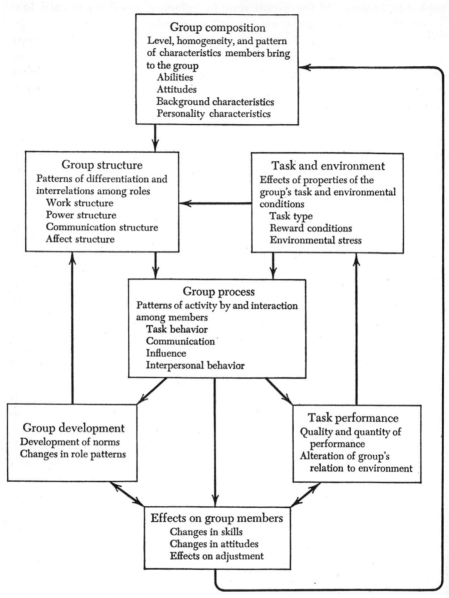

FIGURE 4   Expanded Frame of Reference for Analysis of Groups.

cation, and affect) are interdependent (see group structure, in Chapter 8). Special attention was given to a particular aspect of group structure which has received much emphasis in social psychology, namely, leadership and leader behavior in groups (see Chapter 9).

Chapter 10 was devoted to consideration of how these member, group, and environmental variables are manifested in action as group members interact with one another in pursuit of their goals. Chapter 11 was concerned with some of the major consequences of group activity on the group's accomplishment of its goals, on the group itself, and on group members. Here also we discussed how the three kinds of "outcomes" of group activity—effects on task performance, on the group, and on group members—interact with one another to alter the "input" conditions that exist for and affect subsequent behavior of a group.

SUPPLEMENTARY READING

Collections of Readings from Small Group Research

Cartwright, D., & Zander, A. *Group dynamics.* New York: Harper & Row, Publishers, 1960.

    This is an excellent collection of research studies on small groups. The editors provide also a series of integrative chapters at the beginning of each section of the book.

Hare, A. P., *et al.* (Eds.). *Small groups: studies in social interaction.* New York: Alfred A. Knopf, Inc., 1955.

    This excellent collection of small group research studies has several distinctive features: a section on historical and current theories; and an extensive annotated bibliography of small group research.

Maccoby, E. E., Newcomb, T. M., & Hartley, E. L. *Readings in social psychology.* New York: Holt, Rinehart and Winston, Inc., 1958.

    This excellent collection of readings is not limited to the small group area, but includes research articles from a full range of social-psychological problem areas.

Petrullo, L., & Bass, B. M. (Eds.). *Leadership and interpersonal behavior.* New York: Holt, Rinehart and Winston, Inc., 1961.

    This book is perhaps the best recent collection of papers on leadership, with emphasis on diverse theoretical formulations.

Integrative Summaries of Small Group Research

All these references are compilations and syntheses of research findings from small group research or specialized areas of that field. They represent a range of different approaches to classification of small group phenomena, and tend to complement one another.

Annual review of psychology, 1950–1963, vols. 1–14. Chapters on Group Processes and on Attitudes and Opinions.

Argyle, M. *The scientific study of social behavior.* New York: Philosophical Library, Inc., 1957.

Gibb, C. A. Leadership. In G. Lindzey (Ed.), *Handbook of social psychology.* Reading, Mass.: Addison-Wesley Publishing Company, Inc., 1954. Chap. 24.

Hare, A. P. *Handbook of small group research.* New York: The Free Press of Glencoe, 1962.

Kelley, H. H., & Thibaut, J. W. Experimental studies of group problem solving and process. In G. Lindzey (Ed.), *Handbook of social psychology.* Reading, Mass.: Addison-Wesley Publishing Company, Inc., 1954. Chap. 21.

Mann, R. D. A review of the relationships between personality and performance in small groups. *Psychol. Bull.*, 1959, 56, 241–270.

McGrath, J. E. A summary of small group research studies. Arlington: Human Sciences Research, Inc., 1962. [Under contract No. AF 49(638)-256.]

McGrath, J. E., & Altman, I. *Small Groups Research: A Synthesis and Critique of the Field.* New York: Holt, Rinehart and Winston, Inc., in press (1965).

Roseborough, M. E. "Experimental studies of small groups." *Psychol. Bull.*, 1953, 50, 275–303.

Thibaut, J. W., & Kelley, H. H. *The Social Psychology of Groups.* New York: John Wiley & Sons, Inc., 1959.

PART FOUR /

Society and Culture

Society as a social system

By a social system we mean the total structure and functioning of an organized collectivity of people. We earlier defined a group as a role system. A social system is a network of role networks, a system that is composed of role systems. While this definition would apply to many kinds of collectivities—for example, communities, work organizations—in the present context we will limit its use to refer to total societies (such as the United States) or major segments of them (such as the American Negro, the New England area, the American middle class).

By culture we mean "the precipitate of the history of a given society" (Linton, 1945), its tangible and intangible products, including its rituals, practices, language, values, ideology, and norms.

Each individual is born into a society which, as a social system, is an embodiment of a given culture (or an amalgam of several). There may be one common culture underlying two or more different social systems. For example, the cultural heritage of our society has much in common with that of Great Britain, France, Russia, and Germany. Conversely, a given society may carry an inheritance from a combination of several cultures, well integrated with one another or in conflict. For example, the social system of Mexico still shows influences from Spanish, Aztec, French, American, and perhaps other cultures.

Why deal with culture and society in a book on social psychology? Because the behavior of the individual is influenced by characteristics of the social system and culture in which he lives, quite over and above the constitutional factors in his make-up and the direct effects of social objects in his immediate environment. In large part, the social system and culture have their impact on the individual in indirect, symbolic form. That is, people are influenced by symbolic representations of other people, past and present, such as language, norms, values, prescribed rituals or traditions, laws, and mores.

The social system and culture affect the individual because his personality is shaped via the socialization process, which in any given case is as it is by virtue of the culture, the social system, and the individual personalities involved in the socialization process. The individual's attitudes about himself are also shaped in this process. Further, the role relationships in which the individual can and does participate, the manner in which he fulfills his roles, and the sanctions he receives for his role performances are all in part determined by the culture and social system within which he lives. Thus, the culture and the social system affect the development of the individual's personality and his role behavior throughout life. The individual, in turn, perpetuates the culture by transmitting it to the next generation.

CHAPTER 12

/ *Culture and behavior*

It is tempting to assume that behavior which is character-istic of all the people whom we have observed is therefore (1) universal and (2) an inherent part of human nature. The work of cultural anthro-pologists in the past several decades has shown that many forms of behavior do in fact differ considerably from one culture or society to another. As a matter of methodological convenience, much of this work of the anthropologist has been done with relatively small, intact, stable, and primitive societies, although in recent years attempts have been made to study also more modern, complex cultures such as our own. The central point of this work, for our purposes, is that the domain of culturally deter-mined (and therefore learned rather than inherent) patterns of behavior is much broader than a person would suppose if his experience were limited to a single society. If our experience is limited to one or even a few cultures, we must be wary of generalizations about "human nature."

Role prescriptions for age and sex groups

We tend to think of males and females as having dis-tinctly different personalities, or patterns of behavior, over and above the direct physiological differences between the sexes. In general, we tend to assume that men are more dominant, aggressive, and task-oriented than women, while we assume that women are more passive, "sweet," and compassionate. In terms of our society, such a differentiation is probably fairly accurate—so much so, in fact, that men or women who do not fit this picture are often viewed as deviates and somewhat inferior members of their sex.

Margaret Mead, a leading anthropologist, has shown quite convincingly that many male-female differences in behavior which we tend to think of as universal and an inherent part of the male and female nature are actually determined through the social learning process and differ widely from one culture to another (Margaret Mead, 1935). Mead examined the role behaviors associated with (and expected from) males and females in three primitive societies: the Arapesh, the Tchambuli, and the Mundugumor. In the former, she found that both males and females are expected to behave (and do behave) in a relatively passive manner similar to our expectations for the female role. Among the Mundugumor, both males and females act in the dominant, aggressive manner we expect of males in our society. Among the Tchambuli, our male-female role differentiation is reversed; that is, the female is expected to (and does) act in a dominant, aggressive manner while the male is relatively passive and compassionate.

While these societies were deliberately chosen as extreme and opposite examples and while this early work would now be considered as somewhat "primitive" methodologically, the study serves to make the central point that many differences in male-female behavior are role differences and are learned. They are not a part of male or female human nature in the sense of being organically determined.

Mead goes on to develop the hypothesis that there is a relationship between the sharpness of difference in the role expectations for members of the two sexes and the frequency of occurrence of homosexuality in a society. She argues that the more sharply defined the role expectations for a given sex are, the more likely that an individual who is biologically a member of that sex will find the role difficult or impossible to fulfill. Thus, he is forced either to be an inadequate member of his own sex or to identify with (and act like) a member of the other sex. On the other hand, when a wide range of variability is permitted to both males and females, the chances of such incompatibility are less and the need for cross-sex identification is also less. She found that societies (such as the Arapesh) in which there is no sharp cleavage between male and female role expectations are the only societies in which there is no homosexual behavior.

We tend to expect different patterns of behavior from different age groups in our society. Children are expected to act differently from adolescents, young adults, or older adults, and for the most part such differences in behavior occur. Again, we tend to assume that these are "natural" differences associated with the age level and that they are universal. We tend to stigmatize the individual who departs widely from the pattern of behavior expected for his age level. For example, we might decry the "babyish" actions of an adolescent or ridicule the precocity of the child prodigy. Such differences in role expectations for different age groups can have major consequences for the individual.

Here again, such patterns of behavior are not inherent in human nature but rather are a cultural or social phenomenon. For example, we tend to push our children toward growing up. One frequent form of reward, at least among middle-class parents, is some variant of the remark, "My, aren't you getting to be a big boy!" In contrast, the people of Samoa socialize their children in a form that tends to prolong childhood (Margaret Mead, 1928). Samoan children are not expected to grow up, in our sense of taking on more adult levels of responsibility, at the fastest rate possible; they are encouraged not to do so. A major negative sanction of Samoan parents to their children is, "You are presuming beyond your age."

A further important feature of age roles which varies among cultures is how abruptly the individual is expected to pass from one age level to another, and thus how abruptly he is expected to take on new forms of behavior. For example, many societies use the onset of puberty to define the passage from child to woman or man, demanding a major shift in role behavior essentially overnight.

Another important and variable feature of role expectations is their clarity or ambiguity for a given age or sex group. It has been said that one major cause of the apparent difficulty in adjustment of adolescents in our society is that the society demands both adult forms and childlike forms of behavior from its adolescents, and it is not always clear under what circumstances one or the other type of forms applies. Some have argued that the shifts in role expectations for women in our society have generated much role ambiguity and that this has led to widespread difficulties in adjustment.

Kinship systems and orientations toward the child

Societies differ tremendously in the structure of the family and the characteristic orientations of parents toward their children, and such variations have direct consequences for the shaping of the individual.

Most individuals have two families: a family of orientation, in which the individual is born and raised by his parents and with his siblings; and a family of procreation, in which he is one of the adults who beget and raise children. Family organization in different societies show a wide range of variation. For example, in some societies families are patrilineal, the male line of descent determining the clan membership and often the residence, wealth, and/or social status of the family. In others, families are matrilineal, the family "position" being related to the female line of descent. In still others, families are bilateral, the lines of descent of both parents contributing to the family's clan-membership and status. Many societies have extended family systems; that is, the family "unit" is larger than the single pair of adults and their children.

Ours is a bilaterally determined, nuclear (that is, not extended beyond the two parents and their children) type of family organization in which the residence of the new family of procreation is expected to be separate from both the husband's and the wife's family of orientation and in which the locus of responsibility and control for the new family is separated from either family of orientation. While there is much variability among families in our complex society, this is certainly the normative or expected pattern and probably the most frequently occurring pattern. But while this pattern is typical for our society, it is by no means a universal form of family organization for all cultures.

Family organization can affect human behavior in several ways. For one thing, differences in the role structure of the family are associated with differences in the way love and discipline are administered to children. Among the Arapesh, for example, both parents rear the child. In our society there is a tendency for only the two parents, especially the mother, to be closely involved in the rearing of the child. In Samoa, the child is literally reared by all the adults in the extended family—aunts and uncles and grandparents, older brothers and sisters and cousins, as well as both parents. Among the Mundugumor neither parent takes much direct responsibility for rearing the child; he is given minimal attention, just sufficient to serve his biological needs. Among the Hopi Indians (Aberle, 1951) love and discipline are in large part administered by different persons. The eldest maternal uncle administers all major discipline to the male child, while the child's own father is his constant loving companion. In our society, the father is called upon to administer both love and discipline, often in rapid alternation or nearly at the same time.

These differences in the administration of love and discipline, which derive from differences in family structure in different cultures, in turn generate different patterns of role relationships between the child and the significant others in his social environment. With some patterns intense relationships of love and discipline are focused on one person; with other patterns these relationships are separated, love being associated with one person and discipline with another (among the Hopi), or decentralized, extending to a number of persons (in Samoa). Some patterns tend to minimize the administration of love or discipline or both.

These patterns of relationships of love and discipline affect the personality development of the child. For example, the classical Oedipus complex, in which the male child loves the mother and has an ambivalent mixture of love, hate, and fear of the father, is a natural outgrowth of a family organization in which intense relationships of love and discipline are concentrated in the child's two parents, with the father playing a major role as disciplinarian to his sons. Such a pattern might not have been such a central part of Freud's theory of personality development had he made his early observations on patients from a culture such as that of Samoa or of the Hopi.

Another aspect of family which differs among cultures and which has consequences for the child is the pattern of attitudes parents have toward their children. In some cultures adults view children as creatures to be nurtured; in others they view them as creatures to be trained (disciplined). It is to be expected that such differences in parental orientations toward the child will be associated with differences in their behavior toward him, and, consequently, with differences in their impact on him in the socialization process.

Value-orientation patterns

Cultures differ in belief systems—or ideologies or ways of looking at the world—as well as in the more concrete role behaviors. Florence Kluckhohn (1953) has postulated five basic dimensions of value orientations, each with several categories, along which all cultures can be described. She holds that cultures differ from one another in terms of their main pattern on these five dimensions and that the differences have important consequences for other, more concrete aspects of the culture. The five value-orientation dimensions she postulates and the set of categories she specifies for each dimension are:

1. Man's basic nature: man is thought to be basically good, evil, or a mixture of the two. For any of these categories, man's nature can

be thought of as basically immutable or as capable of change during his lifetime.

2. Man's orientation toward time: toward the past, the present, or the future.
3. Man's relationship to nature: subordinate to it, an integral part of it, or master of it.
4. Man's primary purpose in life: being, being-in-becoming (self-actualization), or doing (achievement).
5. Man's primary relationship to his fellow man: individualistic, lineal (family), or collateral (with his peers).

Kluckhohn holds that patterns on these value dimensions differentiate not only one culture from another but also dominant and subordinate value patterns associated with dominant and subordinate role systems within a single complex society. For example, she holds that males and females, middle- and lower-class groups, and various ethnic and religious groups in our society show different characteristic patterns.

One study of respondents from several different cultures (Kluckhohn and Strodtbeck, 1961) supported Kluckhohn's hypotheses of value-orientation differences between cultures. In another study, McGrath (1962b) found value-orientation pattern differences between members of three different American religious faiths and associated differences in aspects of their behavior in interpersonal situations.

Cultures differ in many ways other than in age and sex roles, family patterns, and value orientations. Cultural differences range all the way from fairly general and abstract belief systems or ideologies to very concrete rituals, mores, and customs.

Each culture offers a more or less integrated pattern of beliefs, values, structures, and practices. Within each, there are likely to be elements of the pattern which *seem* to be disruptive or disfunctional. We cannot just transplant one aspect of a culture to eliminate such a disruptive element, however, because the elements of a culture are intricately interrelated. What seems like a disfunctional element may in fact be a logical and inevitable part of a broader pattern that is highly important to the culture. For example, the change in our family structure from an extended-family type of organization in the rural setting of an earlier day to the present form of separate, nuclear family organization was closely related to a number of other changes in economic and social aspects of our society (such as industrialization, transportation improvements, food and medical improvements, changes in age distributions in the populations). To change it back, precipitously, would be disruptive, unless many compensatory changes in other aspects of our social system also occurred.

CHAPTER 13

/ Social structure:
The pattern of the society

Social institutions as complex role systems

At the group level, we noted that the structural pattern of a group depends on which of several structural dimensions are being considered. The same is true at the social-system level. The structure of a society can be described in a number of ways.

Among the classifications of people which are important for many societies are those by: age; sex; race, tribe, clan, or caste; economic or occupational position; religion; educational or achievement level. Each of these corresponds to a position and a set of roles for the individual. Each such role has associated role expectations and role behaviors. Individuals often evaluate themselves and others in terms of how well role behavior fits role expectations. Of course, as in small groups, the individual occupies *all* his positions (structural differentiations) simultaneously. Thus, the individual can be thought of as a "point" in a multidimensional "space" that we call social structure. He has *some* position, with its accompanying roles, within each major portion of the society. The demands of various roles may or may not be compatible.

As a gross form of classification, let us consider the structure of a social system in terms of five major social institutions, each of which represents a major subsystem of the society: the family-kinship system; the economic system; the religious system; the political-military system; and the educational system. In any given social system, these five subsystems may be sharply differentiated, or two or more of them may tend to blend together. For example, the political system can be tied to family or clan membership, or to religious membership; the family system or educational system to the religious system; the political system to the economic system. It is possible, of course, for one system so to predominate that the other four are subordinated to it.

Each of these social institutions represents a complex system of positions. We can distinguish both value-orientation and structural components of social institutions. For example, we can distinguish between our educational norms and values on the one hand; and our educational system, consisting of the set of practices, facilities, and procedures by which formal education is carried out. Similarly, religious values and norms can be distinguished from religious practices. Our society probably has a far more heterogeneous set of religious practices than of religious value orientations.

A given individual has *some* position and a set of role relationships in each social institution. An atheist as well as a clergyman has a denotable position with respect to the religious structures of a society, just as an unemployed person as well as an industrial worker has a denotable position with respect to its economic institutions. When the individual is called upon to act, his multiple positions and roles may place conflicting demands on him in terms of expected role behaviors.

Stratification: Caste and class

One pervasive feature of most if not all social systems is stratification, or a hierarchical gradation, of members or positions. In almost all social systems there is some degree of differentiation among positions in terms of higher-lower, more less powerful, more or less valued. Such differentiation can take either of two general forms: caste or class.

Caste refers to a stratification into distinct, nonoverlapping, relatively immutable categories, usually arranged in a "social hierarchy." Male versus female is such a differentiation in our society. The religious caste system of India is another example.

Class refers to stratification into less distinct categories, with the implication that it is possible for an individual to move from one class to another. The most common usage of "class" is in reference to the so-called socioeconomic class of an individual. In concept, however, we can think of stratification—caste or class—within any of the social institutions. It is possible for an individual to have a high place in one part of a social system and a relatively low place in another. (For example, school teachers are relatively well educated but relatively low in our economic hierarchy.) Most research on stratification has been done on socioeconomic class. Usually, this research carries the implicit assumption that the economic institution is dominant in American life; thus, that the individual's place in this subsystem is all important in determining his over-all "place" in the society.

There have been three basic approaches to the measurement of socioeconomic class: (1) the reputational approach, in which the individual's social class is defined in terms of who he associates with and how he is perceived by other members of his community (see Warner, 1949); (2) the objective approach, in which the individual's social class is defined in terms of objective indices such as education level, occupation, income, and area of residence (see Hollingshead, 1958); and (3) the subjective approach, which defines social class in terms of the individual's own perception of his class membership (see Centers, 1949). While there are some important differences in results obtained from use of these different approaches, for the most part they lead to comparable results.

Warner, working with the reputational approach, has attempted to define six class levels: upper-upper class, lower-upper class, upper-middle class, lower-middle class, upper-lower class, and lower-lower class. He finds that the differences an individual sees between his own class level and the one below him are greatest; those between his class level and the one above him are smallest. Also, the further the individual himself is from any two social classes, the less sharply he defines the difference between them. The criteria an individual uses to distinguish between the class levels above him and those below him are different. People in the classes above the respondent are perceived as being there because of money and "family." Those in classes below him are perceived as being there because of poorer morals and character, notably, lack of effort and responsibility.

Most of the research on the subject of social stratification has been done on the differences between the middle and lower class or between the middle and working class. Warner's sixfold distinction can seldom be utilized when working with relatively small samples in field studies or in sample surveys of large communities because a sufficient number of members of the upper classes can seldom be obtained in a limited sample.

Some consequences of social stratification

Much research attention has been given to the subject of social stratification because it is assumed that the individual's place in society has important effects on his attitudes, values, and behavior, including his behavior in relation to raising his children. We have already noted, in our discussion of groups, that the social class of jurors (as perceived by their fellow jurors) affects their participation and their influence in the jury situation (Strodtbeck *et al.*, 1957). It has also been shown that social class level is related to political attitudes and voting behavior, although more recent studies indicate that such a relationship varies greatly from one presidential election to another (Converse, 1958). The incidence of psychoses, or at least the frequency of hospitalization in public institutions with a diagnosis of psychosis, is higher for the lower class than for the middle class, while the incidence of hospitalization for neuroses is higher for the middle class than for the lower class (Hollingshead, 1958).

By far the greatest number of studies of social class have been devoted to investigating class effects on child-rearing practices. Early studies of differences in child-rearing practices between middle- and lower-class parents, pertaining to child-rearing practices of the 1930s, showed that middle-class parents used more restrictive control, weaned and toilet trained earlier, and put more and earlier emphasis on independence and responsibility training; while lower-class parents stressed impulse control less, were more permissive, and were more likely to utilize physical rather than psychological control techniques (for example, Davis & Havighurst, 1948).

Some years later, a series of studies on child-rearing practices of the late 'forties and early 'fifties showed substantially the reverse of earlier findings, the middle-class parents being the more permissive (for example, Sears *et al.*, 1957). Bronfenbrenner's (1958) careful analysis of these and other studies of social class and child-rearing practices leads him to the conclusion that there has been a real change in child-rearing practices since the middle 'forties, primarily on the part of middle-class parents, who have increased the permissiveness of their child-training activities. Bronfenbrenner concludes that the change may be the result of the spread of recommendations about "proper" child-rearing practices (presumably, the permissive practices that had previously been characteristic of lower-class parents) via governmental agencies and other public media. He hypothesized that middle-class parents are likely to be exposed to, and to accept, such information as guidance in their own child-rearing activities; hence, the change in middle-class child-rearing practices in the direction of increased permissiveness.

Another possible interpretation of the changes in child-rearing practices is that the composition of the middle class has changed because of the increased geographic, educational, and economic mobility in our society since World War II. Thus, many of the parents of today's middle-class families were themselves raised in lower-class families, and may carry with them the attitudes and practices learned in that setting. This latter interpretation, regarding alterations in the composition of the middle class, would also help explain Converse's (1958) findings that the relationship between social class and political behavior has become reduced or obscured in recent elections.

One major conclusion that should be drawn from the studies of the effects of social class is that the social scientist must be doubly cautious in interpreting and generalizing his findings. Relationships within a complex social system, even when firmly established at a given point in time, may or may not continue to hold even in that same society if the social system is undergoing substantial change. Thus, the statement of general laws in the social sciences is a much more tenuous matter (because of the nature of the phenomena being studied) than is the case for the physical sciences.

CHAPTER 14

| Social process: Stability and change

Continuity and change in a complex society

Up to this point we have been implicitly dealing with the question of why there is continuity from one generation to another within a culture. The general answer seems to be that within a common culture and social system, the adult members of any one subsystem (such as one race and class) exhibit highly similar role behaviors toward their children, who thus have much in common in their childhood experience. This in turn leads to much similarity in the developing personalities of those children and to much similarity in their role behaviors when they become adults and parents. In the second generation, child-rearing practices for that segment of the population are similar to those of the previous generation, and the consequences for the third generation of children are also similar. The members of a culture carry its continuity from one generation to another by similarity in the way in which the socialization process is carried out for succeeding generations.

But our discussion of social class, as well as general observation of our society, indicates that our social system is undergoing rapid change rather than remaining constant. If the above description of cultural continuity is true, how can we account for social change?

Basically, social change occurs for four reasons: (1) In any large society there is bound to be a wide range of variation in the personalities of parents; thus, there will be a range of variation in their ways of relating to their children and consequent variation in the childhood experience of the next generation. (2) The socialization process is necessarily imperfect, in the sense that even the same behaviors on the part of parents will not have identical effects on different children. Rather, a given set of socialization practices will yield some variation in resulting personality. (3) The external environment of the social system may change, thus leading to changes in the social system itself (for example, the Crusades altered the societies of western Europe; World War II altered our society). This in turn leads to changes in the impact of the social system (via socialization) on the new generation of children. (4) There may be certain facets of a society which, by their nature, inevitably lead to development and change in the social system. Parsons (1960) has called these factors *endogenous forces* for change. He cites the institutionalization of science in our society as an example of such an endogenous force making for change in our current society.

Without question, our society is and has been undergoing rapid change and all four of these sources of change apply. In addition to altering our social system, social change, through changes in the pattern of socialization, will have an impact on the formation of personality in future generations. Let us examine some of the major forces for social change in our society, and then consider their potential impact on the individual.

The nature of social change

We often think of social changes as a series of discrete events, for example, the invention of the steam engine, the cracking of the atom. This conception of change suggests that the particular invention or event occurred *sui generis,* without history. Often it also implies that the full impact of the event occurs all at once and more or less immediately. This conception of the nature of social change overlooks the basic continuity of change itself.

History is cumulative. Events do not just happen in a historical and situational vacuum. They occur in a context, the context of existing conditions, needs, and possibilities of the social system within which they take place. Furthermore, events do not just happen and have a denotable set of immediate effects. Rather, the effects of any given event tend to ramify by interacting with the effects of other events and play a part in shaping a whole range of subsequent changes without being the sole cause of those changes.

These points can be illustrated by considering the invention of the automobile around the turn of the twentieth century. The invention of the automobile (and probably most other similar inventions) was not so much a creative breakthrough by an inventive genius as the culmination of a set of prior conditions to fulfill a social *need*. A workable automobile of our present type could only be invented when a number of technological conditions existed: there had to *be* an internal combustion engine and a technology able to process and fashion metals and provide fuel; in fact, the invention of the automobile depended directly on the invention of the wheel. The successful development of the automobile required also the existence of certain social conditions: a need for improvements in land transportation and the desire to go greater distances faster; norms favoring or at least tolerating changes; a positive valuing of new things, progress; and willingness to change traditional ways. Leonardo da Vinci had the *idea* of an auto-mobile (a self-powered machine). He could not invent one, however, because neither the required level of supporting technology nor the appropriate social conditions existed.

Similarly, the effects of the development of the automobile are continuous and a part of the social context. The automobile did not produce all, or even many, of its effects overnight. By 1910, or even 1920, the effects were fairly small. By 1960, tremendous changes had come about, partly because of the automobile. Whole new industries and crafts, not only those directly involved in auto production but also those related to the steel, rubber, and oil industries, were created and/or fostered. The means of waging wars and the scope or scale of wars were changed through major improvements in air, land, and sea transportation. The geographic distribution of people was changed directly, due to greater mobility with the automobile. It was changed indirectly, too, because improved agricultural technology and improved transportation of goods made it both *possible and necessary* (due to the change in the relative importance of farm labor and industrial labor) that we shift from a rural-agricultural to an urban-industrial society. The automobile also changed America's morals, especially by the changes in our patterns of courtship which it facilitated.

It is obvious, of course, that these changes did not arise *solely* from the development of the automobile. Many other technical and social changes occurred as preconditions for these changes. Actually, we could just as well credit these changes to the invention of the wheel or to the discovery of efficient metal-refining processes as to the invention of the automobile. This is precisely the point: social change is a *process*, not a series of discrete events.

The events of today are rooted in current conditions that arose from previous events. And there is a *time lag* between the occurrence of any given event and its full impact on the social system. The impact of technological changes seems to be reflected much more rapidly in our technological and economic institutions than in the social, educational, political, and other aspects of our social system. This difference in the rate of social change for different aspects of our society has been termed *cultural lag.*

From this view of social change, it is clear that the major shape of our society in the future will depend largely on events that happened some time ago, much less so on events and decisions of tomorrow. The current concern with our "population explosion" is a good case in point. Enrollment in our schools and colleges, as well as the unemployment rolls, are and will continue to swell at a rapid rate. *This was totally predictable* from events that took place in the 1940s along with our previously reduced birth rate in the 1930s. Furthermore, there is no policy which we can adopt in 1965 that will change the population figures for 1968 enrollments (assuming that mass murder is ruled out). However, we can very much affect the population figures for 1985 by policies which we, individually or collectively, can adopt now. In short, conditions of today derive from the past, and actions of today have consequences in the future, because social change is a continuous process.

Social change in modern American society

FORCES MAKING FOR CHANGE IN MODERN AMERICAN SOCIETY

One major basis for change in our current society is its size and complexity. First, our social system is built upon a heterogeneity of ethnic groups in various stages of integration. Thus, a given child is likely to be exposed to a range of divergent cultural influences. The rapid industrialization that we have undergone in this century has vastly changed the size and scope of our economy and our way of life. Along with this increase in size has come a great increase in specialization in all aspects of our social system—a much more complex differentiation of role systems. A given individual is now a role participant in many more differentiated role systems, which are intricately interrelated. Parsons terms this a "pluralistic" society, indicating that individuals tend to be highly differentiated one from another in the set of role relationships in which they participate. This view contrasts with the concept of a "mass" society, which implies that individuals tend to be highly undifferentiated one from another. (See Parsons, 1960, for further discussion of this and subsequent points.)

A second feature of our society which is related to its rate of change is that we seem to have a "norm" for change. Our whole history is one of development and expansion, first in geographic terms, later in commercial terms, still later in terms of technical and scientific development. That "progress is good" seems to be a basic value for us, and change is often considered synonymous with progress. Our child-rearing values seem to focus not so much on raising the child to be like his parents, as would be typical for a more tradition-oriented society, but on raising the child to exceed his parents in level of education, in economic success, and in social position.

A third feature, related to the first two, is an upgrading of competence requirements in all areas of our society. As competence requirements increase, the requirements for skill and training also increase. The level of education that makes an individual acceptably well-educated now is higher than it was a generation ago. The same is true regarding occupational training and even "personality training." Parsons holds that along with this upgrading of competence requirements has come a generalization of values. That is, underlying values or rules for behavior tend to be applied universalistically, rather than particularistically, in many more areas than before. What is true or fair or just for ourselves and people "close" to us comes to be seen as equally true, fair, and just for people in all segments of the society. Parsons sees Kennedy's election in 1960 as a big step in institutionalizing a universal value with respect to the relation of religious beliefs to political affairs. A similar comment might be made about the success of the current movement for civil rights for Negroes.

Mass education is both a consequence of, and a force for, social change. The rapid development of our technology, leading to a tremendous upgrading in competence requirements, has produced the requirement of more and better education for all members of the society. Even the degree of automation which we have already experienced, and which is but the beginning of a vast set of changes in our modes of production and distribution of goods, has created a serious problem of "structural unemployment" (i.e., unemployment due to a misfit between the skills available on the labor market and the skills in demand in the economy). We already need more people than are available with higher levels of education and training to support the technology; and we already have more people at lower levels of education and training than can be used in our current technology. Thus, much higher levels of education and training for a bigger proportion of our population is no longer a luxury to be desired for humanitarian reasons but is now a stark economic necessity. At the same time, the rapid increase in mass education that we have experienced, along with the rapid development of better means of communication, serves to quicken the effects of events or new ideas, and thus to speed the process of social change.

BASES OF TENSION IN MODERN AMERICAN SOCIETY

A number of contrasting views exist on what are the major problems or tensions in current American society. Mills (1956) holds that the central fact is the emergence of a single, monolithic "power elite" and a concomitant "massification" of all the rest of society. Riesman (1950), Whyte (1957), and other writers see the major problem as one of increasing conformity and a "de-individualizing" process. Most of these views carry the implication that the basic problem is one of too much similarity, conformity, and lack of individuality on the part of most members of the society.

Parsons (1960) holds a contrasting view. He believes that the major basis for tension in our society is a polarization along an axis of change versus resistance to change. He calls the "progressive" or forward edge of the movement for change the "instrumental activists." The forces that resist change represent various groups whose position would be undercut by changes. For example, rural groups have represented resistance forces, in terms of both economic and political changes. Small business as opposed to "services" now represents forces against social and economic changes. Organized labor, which was once aligned with the forward edge of the movement for social, political, and economic changes, has become a major force resisting automation and other changes in the economic system.

Parsons feels that there is no longer, if there ever was, a polarization in terms of social class. If anything, the polarization is along occupational lines, but there is no single, monolithic elite. He sees several elites: a managerial elite, including business, government, the military and academic institutions; a professional elite; a cultural elite, including those with technical, intellectual, and other competences; a fiduciary-legal elite; and a political elite.

Power is distributed between the private and the public, or governmental, sectors of the society. In the private sector, the instrumental activists have power by virtue of their "technical" competences. In the governmental sector, power is embedded in the forces resisting change (such as the rural–urban vote inequality; the key committee positions held by conservatives of both parties in Congress). Parsons believes that the political parties are not now class differentiated, if they ever were. For example, more than 50 percent of labor voted for Eisenhower in 1956.

Rather, he believes, the two political parties are each internally polarized on the activist-resistance axis.

Such polarization and consequent tension are inherent in our kind of complex, pluralistic social system. Further, Parsons believes that the two sides will not clash directly in the political-power area. In a pluralistic society, affiliations are so cross-cut and ramified, and values so generalized, that it is unlikely that this complex set of allegiances will become polarized on a single content-issue to produce a political power clash. Something of this order apparently occurred, regarding the slavery issue, as a prelude to the Civil War. Parsons feels that it is far less likely now, because of the vastly increased complexity and role differentiation of our society.

Thus, Parsons' view is that the main tension in our society arises from complex and conflicting roles for the individual, rather than from too much similarity or "massification" of the individual. Furthermore, he sees that very complexity of role structure as the major bulwark against both the emergence of a single, monolithic elite and the onset of a major internal power clash.

There is considerable evidence, of a general sort, in support of each position, and it is by no means clear that the views are directly opposed and mutually exclusive alternatives. To the extent that either or both of these views of trends in our society are correct, they have important and differing consequences for the individual.

Social change and the individual

Rapid social change can have several different kinds of consequences for the individual. Durkheim (1897), an early French sociologist, felt that the industrial revolution and subsequent social change had led to "anomie" or "normlessness" on the part of many individuals. That is, individuals whose attitudes and rules of behavior had been learned in a social context that was now greatly changed found themselves without anchors or guides in the new social system in which they lived. Durkheim found this state of affairs to be related to increases in the suicide rate. Later scholars such as Riesman (1950) and Whyte (1957) see essentially this state of change and anomie as leading to adoption of a "social ethic," in which the individual governs his behavior by what he thinks others believe and expect of him. This in turn leads to an increase in conformity, a decrease in individuality, and a general "massification" of the society.

Parsons' view, and the view implied by the materials on role-performance conflicts in Chapter 11, is that the major consequence of social change for the individual is an increase in conflict due to his allegiance to an increasing number of differentiated groups.

A distinction should be made between those groups of which the individual is formally a member (his membership groups) and groups from which the individual derives support for his beliefs and values (his reference groups). A membership group may be a positive or a negative reference group for the individual. For example, an individual who is in the process of moving from a lower to a higher social class may be a member of the lower class but hold it as a negative reference group (that is, he rejects its norms and values) and hold the attitudes and values of the higher-class group, in which he desires but does not yet have membership, as a positive reference for his behavior. When we speak of multiple allegiances as leading to conflict for the individual, we are talking about the individual's multiple reference groups, not necessarily his membership groups.

The previous discussion on role conflict was in the context of small, face-to-face groups. A prime example is the case of a first-line supervisor in industry who meets conflicting demands on his role behavior from management and his men, both of whom have direct role relationships with him. Reference-group conflict is similar but broader, referring to the case where an individual owes allegiance to any two groups whose values or norms are in opposition. The conflict may be between the differing values of two groups within the same social institution or subsystem, such as the values of different social classes for an individual who is in the process of transition between them. Or the conflict may be between values from entirely different domains of the individual's life, such as conflict between the norms of his political and religious reference groups.

The term "marginal man" was originally coined to refer to first-generation immigrants who were a part of two often conflicting cultures. It can be used in a very general way to refer to any individual who is in transition between two groups and for a time affiliated with the norms and values of both. The term would then apply, for example, to the children of racially mixed marriages or religiously mixed marriages, and to individuals who are upward-mobile in educational terms. The problems of adjustment for the "marginal man," in this broad sense, are similar to the problems resulting from role conflict in the small group context. The individual must choose between, or compromise, the conflicting values of the groups competing for his allegiance. In a sense, this problem is the opposite of anomie. The individual suffers not from a lack of norms or anchors but from too many sets of norms which do not jibe with one another. This also is inherent in a highly differentiated, "pluralistic" society.

What are the prospects for the individual in such a rapidly changing, complex society? Although many of the psychologists, sociologists, and other social scientists who have written on this question have developed rather pessimistic views of man's current state (for example, Riesman 1950; Fromm, 1941; Whyte, 1957; Mills, 1956), each of them has offered some suggestions as to the route to a more optimistic future. None of the suggestions are very convincing, however; the possibilities for the future seem to represent more the hoped for possibility than the logically necessary or highly probable consequences of the current state of affairs as described by these men. Parsons' description of current conditions presents a far less pessimistic picture; furthermore, he sees the complexity itself and the multiple allegiances as functionally useful forces in the social system as well as conflict-producing forces for the individual.

While prediction of things to come is far beyond the scope of this material, it is possible to describe some highly likely directions for continued change in our social system. These directions really represent extrapolations of some already existing trends; in Parsons' terms, they are the continuation of changes due to endogenous forces. Barring a major calamity from outside the social system (such as a nuclear war) and a major political revolution from within, certain directions of change are almost certain to continue at an increasing rate. The exploding rate of advance in all scientific fields will continue, probably increase. With it will come continued advances in technology, thus a continued and increasing differentiation and complexity in our entire social structure. Certain professions and crafts will tend to vanish, as did the blacksmiths and glass blowers some decades ago; they will be replaced by many new fields that are related to current and future technological developments and require higher levels of skill and specialization. These changes will require continually higher levels of competence in all spheres of life, in turn necessitating higher levels of skill and training for the individual. Thus, the trend toward more and better education for more people— young and old—will increase.

The tremendous increase in geographic mobility that has occurred since World War II will necessarily continue, with increasingly effective transportation systems. With this increase will come an expansion of the individual's community of reference, just as the individual's social vistas tended to expand greatly as we moved from a society of isolated, agriculturally based towns to a nation of large industrialized urban centers. A world community of nations similar to our own federation of sovereign states, or even an interplanetary culture, is by no means beyond possibility. Some early steps in this direction have already been taken in Europe and South America, as well as in the United Nations. The increasing effect of mass media will tend to hasten this expansion of the individual's community of reference.

The trend toward larger units of government and toward a greater degree of governmental regulation of the economic spheres of life will probably increase as a consequence of the increasing size and complexity of our society. This factor, plus an upward leveling in the economic sphere due to the increased power of organized labor, plus the upward social and economic force of increased mass education, all will tend to restrict stratification of the society at least in terms of socioeconomic class differences as we now know them. These factors, along with Parsons' generalization of values, will tend to reduce existing caste or class distinctions based on race, sex, religion, and similar demographic variables. If anything, we will tend to develop a stratification based on education and/or technical competence, rather than on either demographic variables or economic status.

These directions of change seem highly probable, if not inevitable. The rate at which they will occur will depend on the balance of forces along Parsons' polarization of activist versus resistance groups and on the occurrence of events that tend to divert and slow the process temporarily.

Whether these particular directions of change occur or not, one thing that seems almost certain is that there will be rapid and major changes in our social system. These changes will in turn be reflected in changes in the socialization process by which the personalities of the next generation are shaped. (Consider, for example, the potential effect on the child's social learning of substantial exposure to television. Increased educational facilities and mass media in part increase the number and variation of "agents" who participate in the child's socialization.) These changes in socialization, as well as changes in the society's role systems, will make for changes in the roles the new generation will occupy and in the way in which they will fulfill those roles.

SUPPLEMENTARY READING

Bendix, R., & Lipset, S. M. *Class, status and power.* New York: The Free Press of Glencoe, 1953.

Goldschmidt, W. *Man's way.* New York: Holt, Rinehart and Winston, Inc., 1959.

Goldschmidt, W. (Ed.). *Exploring the ways of mankind.* New York: Holt, Rinehart and Winston, Inc., 1960.

Kluckhohn, C. Culture and behavior. In G. Lindzey (Ed.), *Handbook of social psychology.* Reading, Mass.: Addison-Wesley Publishing Company, Inc., 1954. Chap. 25.

Kluckhohn, C., Murray, H. A., & Schneider, D. M. (Eds.). *Personality in nature, society, and culture* (2nd ed.). New York: Alfred A. Knopf, Inc., 1953. Especially readings by:

Benedict, R. Continuities and discontinuities in cultural conditioning, pp. 522–531.

Davis, A. American status systems and the socialization of the child, pp. 567–576.

Davis, A., & Havighurst, R. J. Social class and color differences in child-rearing, pp. 308–320.

Erikson, E. H. Growth and crises of the "healthy personality," pp. 185–225.

Kluckhohn, Florence R. Dominant and variant value orientations, pp. 342–360.

Merton, R. K. Bureaucratic structure and personality, pp. 376–385.

Parsons, T. Age and sex in the social structure of the United States, pp. 363–375.

Maccoby, E. E., Newcomb, T. M., & Hartley, E. L. (Eds.). *Readings in social psychology*. New York: Holt, Rinehart and Winston, Inc., 1958. Especially readings by:

Bronfenbrenner, U. Socialization and social class through time and space, pp. 400–424.

Charters, W. W., Jr., & Newcomb, T. M. Some attitudinal effects of experimentally increased salience of a membership group, pp. 276–280.

Davis, A., Gardner, B. B., & Gardner, M. R. The class system of the white caste, pp. 371–378.

Deutsch, M., & Collins, M. E. The effect of public policy in housing projects upon interracial attitudes, pp. 612–622.

Hollingshead, A. B. Factors associated with prevalence of mental illness, pp. 425–436.

Mead, Margaret. Adolescence in primitive and modern society, pp. 341–349.

Star, S. A., Williams, R. M., Jr., & Stouffer, S. A. Negro infantry platoons in white companies, pp. 596–601.

Williams, R. M., Jr. Religion, value orientations, and intergroup conflict, pp. 647–654.

PART FIVE /

The Interplay of
Individual, Group, and
Total Society

Thus far we have presented a number of important social-psychological concepts, as well as certain concepts that are "strictly" psychological or "strictly" sociological. We have proceeded analytically, introducing and discussing different concepts and topics as if they were more or less separate and distinct. Such a treatment clarifies presentation, but it leaves us the equally important task of showing how these concepts are related to one another and how collectively they bear on our central problem, namely, analysis of how human behavior is influenced by and simultaneously influences the social environment. This final chapter is devoted to that integrative task.

It will not be possible, of course, to relate all the concepts we have treated in the book (much less all the important concepts of the field of social psychology) within the confines of a single chapter. Rather, our integration will be selective and will attempt primarily to illustrate how concepts from the different levels—individual, group, and society—interlace to form the complex network of social behavior.

CHAPTER 15

/ Social psychology
and the prediction of
human behavior

The science of social psychology is based on the assumption that human behavior is potentially predictable—though not necessarily totally predictable. Several things about that assumption should be clear by now. First, while considerable progress has been made during the relatively short history of scientific social psychology, we are still far from being able to make very refined predictions about human behavior. Second, the prediction of even relatively simple forms of human behavior will require very complex formulations—formulations probably far more complex than those that physical scientists use to predict the trajectory of falling bodies or the movements of molecules of a gas.

The complexity of formulation necessary for adequate prediction of human behavior gives rise to the problem to which this chapter is devoted, namely, analysis of key social psychological concepts as they operate in an interdependent complex to influence human behavior. The behavior of a particular human being occurs, for the most part, in an interpersonal context, in groups. That behavior is affected by factors the individual brings with him to the group (his attitudes, motives, ways of perceiving), and his group experiences in turn help shape the individual's attitudes, perceptions, and personality. The individual himself and the groups in which he participates are both embedded in a total society and culture. The social and cultural environment help shape the experience of the individual in several ways: (1) by structuring the role behaviors of those who have influence on the individual in the process of socialization or personality development; (2) by structuring the positions and roles available to and required of the individual, and the expectations for his performance in those roles; and (3) by structuring the meanings of the situations within which the individual is behaving. The interplay of influences from these three levels—individual, group, and total society— is the focus of this chapter.

Personality

Our central theme has been that *if* human behavior is to be understood and predicted, this must be done from information about the *human organism acting in an environment*. It is the interplay between the *organism* (including all that is biologically given as well as all the past modifications of the organism via learning) and the *situation* (including and especially the interpersonal aspects of the situation, as perceived by the organism) that accounts for human behavior.

Much of what we mean by the "organism" is subsumed in the concept of "personality"—the individual's unique, persistent, dynamic organization of behavior. Where does personality come from? It is the *resultant* organization of all the individual's *learned* behavior patterns. Learning occurs through both associative processes and reinforcement processes. The process of learning is, of course, always *limited by* the biological capabilities of the species and of the particular member of that species, and by the existing level of biological maturation of the organism at any particular time. But at the same time, *what* is learned, and how the results of that learning are organized, is *channeled by* the interplay between the organism and its environment. We cannot learn to perform beyond our inherent capacities; we may or may not learn to perform up to them.

Learning takes place in interaction with the environment, including the *social* aspects of that environment. By social aspects of the environment we mean not only the behavior of other "real and present" human beings in direct interaction but also the products of past human behavior, tangible and intangible. These products include language (spoken and written), along with the concepts, values, and attitudes about the surrounding world which exist in and are transmitted through that language. It also includes the physical artifacts (automobiles, election booths, newspapers, corn fields, air conditioners) that are the resultant of the accumulated past history of the people who form the organism's social environment. In short, the products of past human behavior comprise the culture and the social system of which the individual is a part.

Thus, the environmental context which shapes a given organism is itself conditioned by the cumulative past learnings of the people who make up that environment. This shaping of the individual can be called "socialization" from the point of view of the society, "child-rearing" from the point of view of the family group, and "personality development" from the point of view of the individual. It is central to the development of the organism and the channeling of his subsequent behavior.

The individual's behavior is in part determined by his personality. That is, each person reacts to the world around him in ways that reflect his own unique, learned, persistent organization of behavior. Hence, we should be able to predict human behavior from knowledge about individual personality. And indeed we can—but only in a gross way. For example, we often can make predictions of behavior for people in general but not for John Smith in particular; and we can predict behavior under a particular set of conditions (for example, under highly stressful conditions) but not under a broader range of conditions which operate to influence John Smith's everyday behavior.

There are at least two crucial reasons why we cannot make detailed predictions of behavior on the basis of our knowledge of individual personality. First, it is likely that the fundamental (genotypical) concepts in terms of which human personality can best be conceptualized have not yet been identified. (We may be in the pre-Mendeleev period, in which we are searching for the elements but have not as yet developed concepts analogous to "valence" and "atomic weight" and "electron.") Further theoretical and empirical efforts should, in time, overcome this limitation.

It is worth noting that consideration of the fundamental structure and processes involved in human personality takes us to a kind of limit or boundary of our subject matter where the field of social psychology merges with another field, the psychology of personality. To keep a reasonably consistent focus on our subject matter, we have only touched the territory of that neighboring science, just as we have only touched briefly on topics at the boundaries of the sciences of sociology and anthropology.

The second reason we cannot make detailed predictions about individual behavior from information about individual personality is that personality is not the only important source affecting that behavior. Human behavior is affected by relatively stable patterning of relationships with other people—role relationships as we have called them—which tend to shape the behavior of the role incumbent regardless of that person's unique personality. We will next review how such role relationships relate to personality and the prediction of human behavior.

Role relationships

One important aspect of the socialization or shaping process is that the individual learns the culturally defined, "proper" ways of relating to other people. We have called relationships between persons *role relationships,* and have noted that they carry more or less well defined sets of expectations for how the individuals in those roles should behave vis-à-vis one another. A role incumbent learns a set of expectations for his *own* behavior as well as for the behavior of the person(s) on the other end of his role relationships. These role expectations are crucial for understanding human interaction, because they represent the learned guides and standards toward which the individual orients his own interactive behavior and in terms of which that behavior is evaluated by himself as well as by others.

An individual inevitably becomes a participant in a number of role relationships. Some of these role relationships are based on the individual's *positions* within various narrowly defined groups or sets of people (such as, the husband-to-wife relationship in a particular family; the boss-to secretary relationship in a particular office); they have meaning only with respect to that particular group. Other role relationships are based on the individual's positions within a broad community (for example, the child-to-adult role; the woman-to-man role; the Negro-to-white role). Generally, role expectations for the latter type of broad, institutionalized roles are more general and less detailed than the expectations associated with the former type of group-based roles. Thus, when John Smith relates to any adult female, he behaves to some extent with reference to his perceptions of the role expectations for male-female relationships. This holds whether the female on the other end of the relationship is his wife, his secretary, a female business client, or a waitress in a restaurant. His behavior is further constrained, or channeled, by a more delineated set of role expectations, however, depending upon which of these females are involved in the role relationship. Thus, while there is some similarity in John's behavior toward his wife, his secretary, and various other women, there are likely to be some striking differences too.

Role behaviors are not idiosyncratic. That is, there is much in common between John Smith's behavior toward his wife and the husband-to-wife behavior of many other men (at least, men who are similar to John in age, social background, education, as we shall see later). In fact, some features of the behavior of John Smith toward Mrs. Smith are more like the behavior of Mike Jones toward Mrs. Jones than they are like the behavior of

John Smith toward Miss Johnson, his secretary. Role expectations for husband-to-wife behavior are learned and widely shared—that is, held by most members of a social community—and they differ from role expectations for boss-to-secretary behavior, even though these expectations have a common segment (also learned and shared within a social community) based on the male-to-female role.

But the personality of the individual, which is his unique and persistent organization of behavior, continues to influence behavior to some extent regardless of the particular role relationships involved. Thus, John Smith's behavior in relation to *all* other people—wife, secretary, waitress, male coworker, son—will include certain features that do not change and marks his behavior as uniquely his own. For example, John Smith may tend to be dominating (or, in Schutz' terms, he may have a high need to give "control"). He is likely to exhibit this dominance tendency in *all* his relationships with other people. Thus, he will act in a dominating manner vis-à-vis his wife, secretary, coworkers, and others. Still, the ways in which he exhibits dominance will vary as he interacts in different role relationships.

The situation and past history

We have indicated three major sources of influence on the behavior of a given person in a given role relationship (John Smith's behavior toward his wife). These are: (1) his personality—learned and uniquely his own—which plays a part in all his interpersonal behavior; (2) his role expectations regarding "proper" male-to-female behavior—learned and widely shared within a community—which influence his behavior toward his wife, his secretary, and other females; and (3) his role expectations regarding "proper" husband-to-wife behavior—also learned and widely shared—which affect his behavior only toward his wife. Adequate prediction of John Smith's behavior toward his wife must take into account at least two further sources of influence.

One further source of influence on individual behavior is the *situation* in which the individual is acting. For example, John Smith may kiss his wife or criticize her. Either of these behaviors would differ greatly even for the same husband-wife pair depending on whether it occurred in public or in privacy. Moreover, John's public kiss when his wife visits him at his office is likely to be far less ardent than his kiss at the equally public airport as he returns home after a long absence. In short, John Smith's behavior vis-à-vis his wife depends on the *situation* (the time, the place, the circumstances) in which he is behaving.

Another further source of influence on individual behavior is the *past history* of a particular role relationship. John Smith's behavior toward his wife is likely to be different after one year of marriage from his behavior after ten years, even in the "same" situation. It could perhaps be argued that such changes are due to changes in personality and in age. Such an argument, however, could not account for differences in the role behavior of John Smith toward his long-time secretary and toward her new replacement. Rather, when a given set of persons continue in a given role relationship over a relatively long time, their complementary role behaviors tend to stabilize and to take on certain features peculiar to the particular relationship between those two particular persons. It is this kind of stabilization of expectations and behavior which leads us to expect better coordination between members of a team who have played together for a long time than between equally talented players who are new to each other as teammates.

Thus, we can *add to* the predictability of human behavior by taking into account the general and specific role relationships involved, the history of the particular role relationship, and the situation in which the behavior is occurring, as well as the personalities of the actors. Even with this complicated formulation, we can predict the behavior of individuals only under specified conditions: that is, in terms of specified classes of situations (public versus private, new versus habitual); in terms of specified types of role relationships (mother-to-child); for specified "types" of persons (middle-class white American); and for specified classes of responses. Within these kinds of limits, however, reasonably accurate predictions of human behavior can be made; these are now, and will perhaps always be, statements of *probability* (the likelihood that certain behaviors will or will not occur under certain conditions) rather than definitive yes/no predictions. It is clear, however, that all the sources of influence we have mentioned play a part in affecting behavior and that we are more likely to improve our predictive capabilities by working from the complex model we have presented than by working solely from knowledge of individual personality. Improvement can come as we add to our store of knowledge about the similarities and differences between different role relationships and different situations, as well as between different personalities; and as we add to our understanding of the factors that contribute to the development of role relationships and interpretations of situations as well as those that contribute to the development of personality.

Many of the factors which play a part in the development of both roles and personality, and in definitions of situations, arise out of the structuring of interpersonal relations not only in the small groups in which the individual is a participant but also in the broader communities (societies) within which both the individual and his small groups are embedded.

We will turn now to consideration of some of the culture-based factors, as they affect our ability to understand and predict human behavior.

Culture

Certain of the individual's roles are thrust upon him rather than selected by him. This is so because all societies *categorize* people on the basis of one or more characteristics, treat people in different categories differently, and expect different behaviors from them. Most societies, for example, consider such characteristics as age, sex, race (or tribe or clan) as important bases for classification of its members, and develop norms about what behavior is appropriate *by* and *toward* persons thus classified. In our culture, for example, it is expected that women are to be treated differently from men, and are to act differently from men, at least for a great many day-to-day situations. Similarly, we expect adult-to-child behavior to differ from adult-to-adult behavior, and child-to-adult behavior to differ from child-to-child behavior, over a range of situations. We have noted that the *particular* patterns of behavior expected on the basis of such culturally defined roles differ from one culture to another. For example, we encourage young children to act in more "adult" ways (to be "responsible"), whereas Samoans (as reported by Margaret Mead, 1928) discourage this kind of behavior. Similarly, we expect men to act more dominantly than women, while the Arapesh (Margaret Mead, 1935) do not expect such differences. In the main, such culture-based expectations are fulfilled, for two related reasons: (1) because social reinforcements or sanctions (rewards or punishments) are applied toward those who do and those who do not perform as expected; and (2) because these broadly shared expectations about behavior are learned and "internalized" as standards, so that in a sense the individual rewards (or punishes) himself for performances that meet (or violate) the learned expectations.

Culturally bound norms (that is, expectations and the sanctions associated with them) affect our definitions of situations as well as our expectations about role relationships. For example, in our culture two good friends may compete against each other fiercely if on opposing teams or even if pitted directly against each other in a boxing match; whereas in another situation, such as at a party or in a job situation, good friends would try very hard not to oppose or defeat each other. We define certain situations as competitive—that is, we expect persons in those situations to try to win, regardless of whom they are opposing. In some other cultures (in Samoa, for example, or among the Zuñi Indians) two friends would not respond competitively in such game situations; in fact, they would probably refuse to participate in such situations. In those societies, there are strongly supported (sanctioned) norms *against* individual self-enhancement by defeating an opponent. It is "improper" to try to outrace or outplay or outdo an opponent in a contest. (Once again we have reached a boundary between our subject matter, social psychology, and a related field. To explore the question of how cultural differences arise would take us far into the neighboring science of anthropology.)

Thus, the broader cultural setting within which an individual exists, as well as the direct interpersonal setting, affects both the personality development of the individual and his expectations (and those of others) about appropriate behavior. The culture within which we are acting helps shape our interpretations of situations and our expectations about behavior in our role relationships. Hence, knowledge about cultural norms can add to our ability to predict behavior.

Social structure

We must not assume that "the culture" is homogeneous in its impact on all members, especially in complex cultures such as our own. Societies tend to classify members in various ways and to have different expectations about the behavior of members who "belong" in different categories. Thus, the total society tends to become stratified or segmented, in terms of age, sex, race, education, and other bases. Sometimes these strata acquire value orderings; that is, members of a society develop shared attitudes about the relative desirability of the different categories of people. And sometimes such segmentation produces barriers to free communication and interaction between strata, so that the people who are in different segments of the society tend to develop separate communities of interaction. Such barriers exist in our society, for example, between Negroes and whites; between persons of middle- and lower-class backgrounds; between teen-agers, on the one hand, and both children and adults on the other. Isolation of strata of a society, in effect, leads to the development of a series of subsocieties or subcultures. Such subcultures are likely to develop different values, norms, and expectations for behavior, different interpretations of many kinds of situations, and even different languages—because they exist in different worlds and therefore need different structurings of reality to cope with their respective environments.

Thus, it is more directly the values, norms, and expectations of the particular subculture to which an individual belongs rather than expectations of the total culture, which affect the individual's behavior. The child's developing personality is shaped, in the first instance, by interaction with parents who are representatives of certain subcultures and not others (on the basis of their race, religion, educational and economic levels, and other factors). Furthermore, the individual acquires roles based on the positions his subcultures define for him (based on his sex, race, age, and other characteristics). Definitions of positions, and of role relationships based on them, stem basically from the subcultures in which the individual participates, rather than from the total culture. For example, the husband-wife role relationships (expectations for behavior) are different as defined by middle class and lower class, by Negroes and whites, by Mormons, Catholics, and Methodists. Of course, the expectations of all of these subcultures are somewhat influenced by the total culture of which they are a part. In many ways, for example, American Negroes are more like American whites than they are like Negroes who live in Liberia, or Spain, or Haiti. Similarly, middle-class Negroes are in many ways more like middle-class whites than they are like lower-class Negroes. Nevertheless, both social class and race, and many other bases of social stratification, tend to lead to distinct subcultures with differing patterns of behavior and expectations.

Subcultures also shape our definitions of situations. Indeed, the very range and types of situations about which we learn expected ways of behaving vary depending on the subcultures of which we are a part. The adolescent girl raised in a lower-class culture who finds herself suddenly in the midst of a cotillion ball and the upper-class boy who is suddenly confronted with a street-corner brawl would be equally at a loss to know what to do in such a totally strange situation. They literally would have no way of defining the situation so as to apply their learned norms and expectations to guide their behavior. Their past learning, chances are, would not have included any guides or standards for behavior in these types of situations. In contrast, persons of the same sex, age, and native ability as the individuals described but from different subcultural backgrounds, namely, an upper-class subdeb and a city-bred lower-class boy, would have no difficulty in interpreting the situation and in applying learned expectations about their behavior and the behavior of others.

This example illustrates an additional feature of social stratification which affects behavior. Sometimes an individual gets involved in two or more subcultures at the same time, so that he holds competing expectations about behavior in certain situations. This can be illustrated by a person who is moving upward in terms of economic status. He may frequently find himself in situations where his previously learned role behaviors (behaviors learned in the context of his former subculture) no longer apply and the role expectations associated with his new "status" have not yet been adequately learned and internalized. Similarly, we can view many of the adjustment problems of adolescents in our society as essentially due to a shift in subcultures (from that of child to that of near-adult), so that the individual is faced with situations for which he has no established behavioral expectations and/or for which his former role expectations no longer apply.

(Further consideration of the forms of social stratification and mobility, and the conditions under which they arise, would again require explorations beyond the bounds of social psychology, into the realm of the neighboring science of sociology. So, again, we shall redirect our focus to another social-psychological aspect of human behavior.)

Social change

Our discussion of the effects of subcultural shifts suggests a further dimension relating to the sources that influence human interactive behavior, namely, the question of stability and change in the social environment. While we can trace the transmission of cultural (and subcultural) norms from generation to generation in the shaping of personality, the definitions of situations, and the learning of roles, we need to recognize also that we live in a dynamic rather than a static social environment. Cultures and social structures change, bringing about changes in the behavior of their members.

For one thing, the individual himself changes positions throughout his life, and hence is constantly encountering new role relationships to be learned. Some bases for roles, such as age, inevitably change; the child must in time become an adolescent, then an adult, then a senior citizen. With this change come other changes, to a greater or lesser degree, in the roles the person occupies—his possible roles in the economic structure of the society and his possible roles in terms of marriage, parenthood, grandparenthood. Other bases for roles may or may not shift: the individual may or may not alter his educational level; he may or may not obtain job promotions; he may or may not join and participate in various types of organizations. Some bases of stratification, such as sex and race, are relatively immutable. Role change occurs even here, however; while the classification characteristic may be unchangeable, its culturally defined meaning may shift tremendously even within one person's lifetime. Thus, in our society we have seen major shifts in the role of women (that is, in our expectations about their behavior) and in the role relationships of Negroes and whites toward one another, even within the last decade. When such role relationships change, even though no one changes in his position (from woman to man, or from Negro to white), such changes have an influence on the behavior of all occupants of all the roles involved.

Cultures change in other ways as well. Previously distinct subcultures sometimes become merged. One could argue, for example, that differences between economically based classes in our society have tended to diminish because of economic leveling, broader access to higher education, and broader access to mass media of communication. Conversely, new subcultures tend to develop to meet new conditions. The emergence of a "teen culture" in our society, with its own norms, values, dress, and language, is a case in point. In an earlier era, the age-based progression of a person's life passed rather directly from child to man. In large part, a child became a man when he could do a man's work (enter into the economic structure of the community) and when he married. In our current society, many forces operate to *delay* the full attainment of adulthood for many years beyond the organism's biological maturity. A much longer period of training is required before the individual can adequately play a role in the economic structure (at least for the roles aspired to by members of some of our subcultures), and lack of economic viability often requires a delay in marriage. Persons receiving extended training before entering the economic structure—who are biologically mature but not socially mature as our culture defines such maturity—are neither children nor adults. As these changes in our culture have taken place, the adolescent has become more and more recognized, by himself as well as by others, as a special age group with a special (though poorly defined) position in the society. Thus, teen-agers have become a differentiated segment of our society: they constitute a distinctive subculture, which has its own specialized norms and behavioral expectations for the special sets of role relationships which exist in that subculture.

All such changes in a society bring with them changes in the behavior of members of that society—resulting from changes in personality development, as well as changes in the set of roles which exist, in role expectations for those roles, and in definitions of situations. John Smith certainly behaves differently toward his teen-age son today than he would have behaved as father of a teen-age boy thirty years ago—even if John and the boy had each had the "same" personalities as they have today and had been acting in the "same" situation. John's behavior would have been different also toward his wife, toward a female or Negro applicant for a high-level position in his firm, and toward persons in many other role relationships. Just as an individual's movement within a social system may place him in conflict situations for which he does not have adequate guides for his behavior, so changes in the social system, which bring changes in role relationships and in definitions of situations, may pose ambiguous situations for which the individual is not equipped. New situations and new role relationships require the learning of new role expectations. Thus, any attempt to predict the behavior of John Smith in a particular set of circumstances must take into account the changing culture within which John exists and acts.

The importance of subjective experience

Throughout this discussion of the effects of personality, roles, situations, cultures, and social structure on our ability to predict behavior, we have been talking as if our main focus were on overt and directly observable motor activities of John Smith and his various role partners. We have been talking, too, as if role expectations for a particular role, as understood by most members of a community or as viewed by an "objective" observer, were necessarily the same as the role expectations as John Smith understood them. Neither of these conditions is true. John Smith's behavior toward his wife is guided by role expectations for male-female relations and for husband-wife relations, and by the culturally defined meaning of the behavior situation—but only as these expectations and definitions are *perceived by John*. While norms and role expectations are widely shared within a community, they may or may not be accurately perceived by any given member. Thus, individuals often behave with reference to role expectations that are no longer generally shared by others in related roles, simply because they are not aware that there has been a change. Similarly, an individual is not likely to act differently in two "different" situations if he does not perceive the situations as different, even if other persons involved in the situations do make that distinction. Inaccuracies in perception, therefore, give rise to another array of problems of adjustment for the individual, and constitute another source of influence on his behavior.

Furthermore, the individual's overt motor behavior does not constitute all, and probably not even the most important part, of the individual's behavior that is worthy of our scientific efforts to understand and predict. We are also concerned with understanding and predicting many aspects of human subjective experience—patterns of motives, values, and attitudes—whether or not there is a one-to-one translation between the experience and observable, overt behavior. Thus, the individual's personality, his role expectations, and his perceptions of the situation probably tell us more about his *predispositions* toward behavior than they tell us about actual overt behavior. For example, John Smith might be fully aware of the shared role expectations against arguing with his wife in public, and might have no wish to violate those expectations, and nevertheless end up in the midst of a public argument with her. Many other factors, including the intrusions of other persons into a particular role relationship, unanticipated changes in situation or in needs, and "recurrent themes" from past events involving the two parties may alter conditions so that John and his wife violate their own strongly held and shared expectations for their own behavior and the behavior of the other.

In large part, our efforts to predict human behavior focus on the covert, "predispositional" side of behavior. In much of social psychology, there is the implicit assumption that these "internal states" of the organism—if we could measure them adequately—are the more stable and predictable aspects of human behavior; whereas overt behavior is much more affected by essentially chance events in the environment. Thus, it is the subjective experience of the individual and modifications of that experience via the impact of features of the social environment which are of central concern in our endeavors to understand and predict human behavior. The individual's positions, roles, subcultural norms, and values, and the group pressures for conformity, socialization practices, and interpersonal relations to which he is exposed, have meaning within our inquiry only as they affect his motives, attitudes, perceptions, and predispositions to act—in short, as they affect the systematic (and hence predictable) aspects of his behavior.

/ References

Aberle, D. F. The psycho-social analysis of a Hopi life-history. *Comp. Psychol. Monogr.*, 1951, *21*, No. 1.

Allport, F. H. The influence of the group upon association and thought. *J. exp. Psychol.*, 1920, *3*, 159–182.

Altman, I., & McGinnies, E. Interpersonal perception and communication in discussion groups of varied attitudinal composition. *J. abnorm. soc. Psychol.*, 1960, *60*, 390–395.

Asch, S. E. Studies of independence and conformity: I. A minority of one against a unanimous majority. *Psychol. Monogr.*, 1956, *70*, No. 9 (Whole No. 416).

Back, K. W. Influence through social communication. *J. abnorm. soc. Psychol.*, 1951, *46*, 9–23.

Back, K. W. Power, influence and pattern of communication. In L. Petrullo, & B. M. Bass (Eds.), *Leadership and interpersonal behavior.* New York: Holt, Rinehart and Winston, Inc., 1961.

Bales, R. F. *Interaction process analysis: A method for the study of small groups.* Reading, Mass.: Addison-Wesley Publishing Company, Inc., 1950.

Bales, R. F., & Slater, P. Role differentiation in small decision-making groups. In T. Parsons, *et al.* (Eds.), *Family, socialization, and interaction process.* New York: The Free Press of Glencoe, 1955, 259–306.

Bales, R. F., & Strodtbeck, F. L. Phases in group problem solving. *J. abnorm. soc. Psychol.*, 1951, *46*, 485–495.

Bavelas, A. Communication patterns in task groups. *J. accoust. Soc. Amer.*, 1950, *22*, 725–730.

Berrien, F. K. Homeostasis theory of groups—implications for leadership. In L. Petrullo, & B. M. Bass (Eds.), *Leadership and interpersonal behavior.* New York: Holt, Rinehart and Winston, Inc., 1961, 82–99.

Bronfenbrenner, U. Socialization and social class through time and space. In E. E. Maccoby, T. M. Newcomb, & E. L. Hartley (Eds.), *Readings in social psychology.* New York: Holt, Rinehart and Winston, Inc., 1958, 400–424.

Bruner, J. S., & Goodman, C. C. Value and need as organizing factors in perception. *J. abnorm. soc. Psychol.,* 1947, *42,* 33–44.

Carter, L. F., *et al.* A further investigation of the criteria of leadership. *J. abnorm. soc. Psychol.,* 1950, *45,* 350–358.

Carter, L. F., *et al.* A note on a new technique of interaction recording. *J. abnorm. soc. Psychol.,* 1951, *46,* 258–260.

Centers, R. *The psychology of social classes,* Princeton, N.J.: Princeton University Press, 1949.

Chapple, E. D. Measuring human relations: An introduction to the study of interaction of individuals. *Genet. Psychol. Monogr.,* 1940, *22,* 3–147.

Coch, L., & French, J. R. P., Jr. Overcoming resistance to change. *Hum. Relat.,* 1948, *1,* 512-532.

Cohen, A. R. Experimental effects of ego defense preference on interpersonal relations. *J. abnorm. soc. Psychol.,* 1956, *52,* 19–27.

Converse, P. E. The shifting role of class in political attitudes and behavior. In E. E. Maccoby, T. M. Newcomb, & E. L. Hartley (Eds.), *Readings in social psychology.* New York: Holt, Rinehart and Winston, Inc., 1958, pp. 388–399.

Cooley, C. H. *Human nature and the social order.* New York: Charles Scribner's Sons, 1902.

Davis, A., & Havighurst, R. J. Social class and color differences in child rearing. *Am. soc. Rev.,* 1948, *11,* 698–710.

Deutsch, M. A theory of cooperation and competition. *Hum. Relat.,* 1949, *2,* 129–152.

Durkheim, E. Suicide (transl. of *Le suicide.* Paris: Falcan, 1897). New York: The Free Press of Glencoe, 1951.

Erikson, E. H. *Childhood and society.* New York: W. W. Norton & Company, Inc., 1950.

Festinger, L., *et al. Social pressures in informal groups: A study of human factors in housing.* New York: Harper & Row, Publishers, 1950.

Festinger, L., & Katz, D. *Research methods in the behavioral sciences.* New York: Holt, Rinehart and Winston, Inc., 1953.

Fiedler, F. E. *Leader attitudes and group effectiveness.* Urbana, Ill.: University of Illinois Press, 1958.

Fiedler, F. E. Leadership and leadership effectiveness traits: A reconceptualization of the leadership trait problem. In L. Petrullo & B. M. Bass (Eds.), *Leadership and interpersonal behavior.* New York: Holt, Rinehart and Winston, Inc., 1961.

Fiedler, F. E. Leader attitudes, group climate, and group creativity. *J. abnorm. soc. Psychol.*, 1962, *65*, 308–318.

Fiedler, F. E., & Meuwese, W. A. T. Leader's contribution to task performance in cohesive and uncohesive groups. *J. abnorm. soc. Psychol.*, 1963, *66*, 83–87.

Fiedler, F. E., *et al.* Quasi-therapeutic relations in small college and military groups. *Psychol. Mongr.*, 1959, *73*, No. 3 (Whole No. 473).

Fielder, F. E., Meuwese, W. A. T., & Oonk, S. An exploratory study of group creativity in laboratory tasks. *Acta Psychol.*, Amsterdam, 1961, *18*, 100–119.

Fouriezos, N., Hutt, M., & Guetzkow, H. Measurement of self-oriented needs in discussion groups. *J. abnorm. soc. Psychol.*, 1950, *45*, 682–690.

French, J. R. P., Jr. A formal theory of social power. *Psychol. Rev.*, 1956, *63*, 181–194.

French, J. R. P., Jr., & Raven, B. The bases of social power. In D. Cartwright (Ed.), *Studies in social power.* Ann Arbor, Mich.: University of Michigan, Institute for Social Research, 1959.

Fromm, E. *Escape from freedom.* New York: Holt, Rinehart and Winston, Inc., 1941.

Gibb, J. R. Defense level and influence potential in small groups. In L. Petrullo, & B. M. Bass (Eds.), *Leadership and interpersonal behavior.* New York: Holt, Rinehart and Winston, Inc., 1961.

Glanzer, M., & Glaser, R. Techniques in the study of group structure: II. Empirical studies of effects of structure in small groups. *Psych. Bull. 58*, 1961, 1–27.

Guetzkow, H., & Simon, H. A. The impact of certain communication nets upon organization and performance in task-oriented groups. *Mgmt. Science*, 1955, *1*, 233–250.

Hall, C. S., & Lindzey, G. *Theories of personality,* New York: John Wiley & Sons, Inc., 1957.

Hare, A. P. A study of interaction and consensus in different sized groups. *Amer. sociol. Rev.* 1952, *17*, 261–267.

Haythorn, W., *et al.* The behavior of authoritarian and equalitarian personalities in groups. *Hum. Relat.*, 1956, *9*, 57–74.

Hemphill, J. K. Situational factors in leadership. *Ohio State University Educ. Res. Monogr.*, 1949, No. 32.

Hemphill, J. K. Why people attempt to lead. In L. Petrullo, & B. M. Bass (Eds.), *Leadership and interpersonal behavior.* New York: Holt, Rinehart and Winston, Inc., 1961.

Hoffman, L. R. Homogeneity of member personality and its effect on group problem-solving. *J. abnorm. soc. Psychol.*, 1959, *58*, 27–32.

Hollingshead, A. B. Factors associated with prevalence of mental illness. In E. E. Maccoby, T. M. Newcomb, & E. L. Hartley (Eds.), *Readings in social psychology,* New York: Holt, Rinehart and Winston, Inc., 1958.

Horney, K. *New ways in psychoanalysis.* New York: W. W. Norton & Company, Inc., 1939.

Hurwitz, J. L., *et al.* Some effects of power on the relations among group members. In D. Cartwright, & A. Zander (Eds.), *Group dynamics—research and theory,* New York: Harper & Row, Publishers, 1960.

Hutchins, E. B., & Fiedler, F. E. Task-oriented and quasi-therapeutic role functions of the leader in small military groups. *Sociometry,* 1960, *23,* 393–406.

Kelley, H. H. Communication in experimentally created hierarchies. *Hum. Relat.,* 1951, *4,* 39–56.

Killian, L. M. The significance of multiple-group membership in disaster. *Amer. J. Sociology,* 1952, *62,* 309–314.

Kluckhohn, Florence. Dominant and variant value orientations. In C. Kluckhohn, H. A. Murray, & D. M. Schneider (Eds.), *Personality in nature, society, and culture.* New York: Alfred A. Knopf, Inc., 1953.

Kluckhohn, Florence, & Strodtbeck, F. L. *Variations in value orientations.* New York: Harper & Row, Publishers, 1961.

Lanzetta, J., & Roby, T. B. Effects of work group structure and certain task variables on group performance. *J. abnorm. soc. Psychol.,* 1956, *53,* 307–314.

Leavitt, H. J. Some effects of certain communication patterns on group performance. *J. abnorm. soc. Psychol.,* 1951, *46,* 38–50.

Levine, R., Chein, I., & Murphy, G. The relation of the intensity of a need to the amount of perceptual distortion, a preliminary report. *J. Psychol.,* 1942, *13,* 283–293.

Linton, R. *The cultural background of personality,* New York: Appleton-Century-Crofts, 1945.

Lippett, R., *et al.* The dynamics of power: A field study of social influence in groups of children. *Hum. Relat.,* 1952, *5,* 37–64.

McClelland, D. C., & Atkinson, J. W. The projective expression of needs: I. The effect of different intensities of the hunger drive on perception. *J. Psychol.,* 1948, *25,* 205–222.

McGrath, J. E. The influence of positive interpersonal relations on adjustment and effectiveness in rifle teams. *J. abnorm. soc. Psychol.,* 1962a, *65,* 365–375.

McGrath, J. E. Value-orientations, personal adjustment, and social behavior of members of three American religious groups. Tech. Rep. No. 15, February, 1962b, Urbana, Ill.

Mead, G. H. *Mind, self and society.* Chicago: University of Chicago Press, 1934.

Mead, Margaret. *Coming of age in Samoa.* New York: William Morrow & Company, Inc., 1928.

Mead, Margaret. *Sex and temperament in three primitive societies.* New York: William Morrow & Company, Inc., 1935.

Mills, C. W. *The power elite.* New York: Oxford University Press, 1956.

Mintz, A. Non-adaptive group behavior. *J. abnorm. soc. Psychol.,* 1951, *46,* 150–159.

Mulder, M. Power and satisfaction in task-oriented groups. *Acta Psychol.,* Amsterdam, 1959, *16,* 178–225.

Mullahy, P. *Oedipus, myth and complex.* New York: Hermitage House, Inc., 1952.

Myers, A. Team competition, success, and the adjustment of group members. *J. abnorm. soc. Psychol.,* 1962, *65,* 325–332.

Newcomb, T. M. *Personality and social change.* New York: Holt, Rinehart and Winston, Inc., 1943.

Newcomb, T. M. *Social Psychology.* New York: Holt, Rinehart and Winston, Inc., 1950.

Newcomb, T. M. An approach to the study of communicative acts. *Psychol. Rev.,* 1953, *4,* 183–214.

Newcomb, T. M. *The acquaintance process.* New York: Holt, Rinehart and Winston, Inc., 1961.

Newcomb, T. M. Attitude development as a function of reference groups. In E. E. Maccoby, T. M. Newcomb, & E. L. Hartley (Eds.), *Readings in social psychology,* New York: Holt, Rinehart and Winston, Inc., 1958, 265–275.

Parsons, T. C. *Structure and process in modern societies.* New York: The Free Press of Glencoe, 1960.

Riesman, D. *The lonely crowd.* New Haven, Conn.: Yale University Press, 1950.

Roby, T. B. The executive function in small groups. In L. Petrullo, & B. M. Bass (Eds.), *Leadership and interpersonal behavior.* New York: Holt, Rinehart and Winston, Inc., 1961.

Rogers, C. R. *Counseling and psychotherapy.* Boston: Houghton Mifflin Company, 1942.

Schachter, S. Deviation, rejection, and communication. *J. abnorm. soc. Psychol.,* 1951, *46,* 190–207.

Schachter, S., *et al.* An experimental study of cohesiveness and productivity. *Hum. Relat.,* 1951, *4,* 229–238.

Schutz, W. C. *FIRO: A three-dimensional theory of interpersonal behavior.* New York: Holt, Rinehart and Winston, Inc., 1958.

Schutz, W. C. The ego, FIRO theory and the leader as completer. In L. Petrullo, & B. M. Bass (Eds.), *Leadership and interpersonal behavior,* New York: Holt, Rinehart and Winston, Inc., 1961.

Sears, R. R., Maccoby, E. E., & Levin, H. *Patterns of child rearing.* New York: Harper & Row, Publishers, 1957.

Selltiz, C., Jahoda, M., Deutsch, M., & Cook, S. W. *Research methods in social relations.* New York: Holt, Rinehart and Wiston, Inc., 1962.

Shaw, Marjorie E. A comparison of individuals and small groups in the rational solution of complex problems. *Amer. J. Psychol.,* 1932, *44,* 491–504.

Shaw, M. E. Some effects of problem complexity upon problem solution efficiency in different communication nets. *J. exp. Psychol.,* 1954, *48,* 211–217.

Shaw, M. E. *Scaling group tasks: A method for dimensional analysis.* Tech. Rep. No. 1, ONR Contract NR 170–266, Nonr 580(11), July 1963.

Steiner, I., & Rajaratnam, N. A model for the comparison of individual and group performance scores. *Behav. Science,* 1961, *6,* 142–147.

Strodtbeck, F. L., *et al.* Social status in jury deliberations. *Amer. sociol. Rev.*, 1957, *22*, 713–719.

Taylor, D. W., *et al.* Does group participation when using brain-storming facilitate or inhibit creative thinking? New Haven, Conn.: Yale University, November, 1957. (Tech. Rep. No. 1, Contract Nonr 60920.)

Taylor, D. W., & Faust, W. L. Twenty questions: Efficiency in problem solving as a function of size of group. *J. exp. Psychol.*, 1952, *44*, 360–368.

Taylor, F. W. *The principles of scientific management.* New York: Harper and Row, Publishers, 1911.

Thelen, H. Techniques for collecting data on interaction. *J. soc. Issues*, 1950, *6*, 77–93.

Thibaut, J. W. An experimental study of the cohesiveness of underprivileged groups. *Hum. Relat.*, 1950, *3*, 251–278.

Thomas, E. J. Effects of facilitative role interdependence on group functioning. *Hum. Relat.*, 1957, *10*, 347–366.

Torrance, E. P. Some consequences of power differences on decision making in permanent and temporary three-man groups. *Res. Stud., Wash. State Coll.*, 1954, *22*, 130–140.

Warner, W. L., Meeker, M., *et. al. Social class in America.* Chicago: Science Research Associates, Inc., 1949.

Whyte, W. H., Jr. *The organization man.* New York: Doubleday & Company, Inc., 1957.

Name Index

Subject Index